White Trash GATHERINGS

*From-Scratch Cooking
for Down-Home Entertaining*

Kendra Bailey Morris

TEN SPEED PRESS
Berkeley | Toronto

This book is dedicated to all the proud White Trashers out there—
and to those who wish they were.

Ten Speed Press
Box 7123
Berkeley, California 94707
www.tenspeed.com

Distributed in Australia by Simon and Schuster Australia, in Canada by Ten Speed Press Canada, in New Zealand by Southern Publishers Group, in South Africa by Real Books, and in the United Kingdom and Europe by Publishers Group UK.

Cover and text design by Katy Brown
Front cover photograph by Kendra Bailey Morris

Library of Congress Cataloging-in-Publication Data
Morris, Kendra Bailey.
   White trash gatherings : from-scratch cooking for down-home entertaining /
Kendra Bailey Morris.
       p. cm.
   Summary: "A guide to entertaining the white trash way, featuring 150
family recipes, photographs, party tips, craft ideas, folk remedies, and
tall tales from a country gal born in West Virginia"—Provided by publisher.
   Includes index.
   ISBN-13: 978-1-58008-774-2
   ISBN-10: 1-58008-774-4
   1. Cookery, American—Southern style. 2. Entertaining. I. Title.
   TX715.2.S68M677 2006
   641.5'975—dc22
                                    2006018226

Printed in Canada

3 4 5 6 7 8 9 10 — 10 09 08 07

CONTENTS

Acknowledgments v

Introduction: Hot Rolls and Sweaty Cooks vi

PART ONE: JUST HAVIN' 'EM OVAH

  1 Squirrel Huntin' and Miss Edythe's Biscuits 2

  2 We Can't Have Dinner without Hors de Voos! 13

  3 Beans, Cornbread, and Politickin' 20

  4 Wash Day Dinners 30

PART TWO: HOLY GATHERIN'S

  5 Why the Ice Cream Social Should Be Made Illegal.................... 38

  6 Wednesday Night Suppers—Fried Chicken and Torpedos 47

  7 After-Church Entertaining—West Virginia Rat Tales................ 55

  8 Christmas Dinner at Granny Boohler's and Grandpa Woody's
House, or Why We Don't Need Manners 62

PART THREE: POTLUCK HEAVEN

  9 Family Reunions—Warring Matriarchs, Shackin' Up,
and Cousin Love.. 74

 10 When in Doubt, Go Whole Hog! 84

 11 Comforting Comforts—Ball Jars and Funeral Cake 93

PART FOUR: CREATIN' YOUR OWN GATHERIN' FROM SCRATCH

 12 Pickin' from the Relish Tray 106

 13 "Real" Salads 109

 14 Killin' and Grillin'—Beef, Pork, and Game 112

 15 Chicken, Turkey, Little Birds, and Other
Fair-Feathered Friends... 121

 16 Headin' Down to Granddaddy's Fishin' Hole 126

 17 Veggie Pickin's and Cannin' 131

 18 Soups, Beans, Breads, and Casseroles—
How a Can of Soup Can Lead to Instant Culinary Genius....... 136

19 Jell-O Salads and Other Jiggly Treats—
    On the Greatness of Suspended Food.. 144
20 Let 'Em Eat Cake!.. 150
21 Fried Pies, Fruit Pies, and Custards 154
22 Candies, Cookies, and Mystery Sweets..................................... 158
23 Boozy Drinks and Church-Friendly Libations.......................... 161

About the Author 166

ACKNOWLEDGMENTS

This book has proven to be the ultimate family gathering. Without the contributions of my grannies, Beulah Bailey (a.k.a. Granny Boohler), Pat Belcher, Charity Wooten, Maw Maw Tiller, and Hazel Wimmer, and my grandpas, Woodrow Bailey, Willard Belcher, Ed Wooten, Center Wooten, and Paw Paw Tiller, the recipes and stories found in this book would never have been brought to life. Your stories as well as your cooking will always live on.

To the late Ernest Matthew Mickler, our pioneer white trasher, your books were an inspiration to me long before I sat down to write one word in your honor. You are a true original.

To my friends who generously donated their cooking and eating time at pig pickin's and gatherings, and with special thanks to Staino and B. Holsten, who are true pit masters in every sense. To the Haney family, Jane and Harold, and to my "sisters" Ellen, Allison, and Janet. We may not be blood, but we will always be kin. Thank you for giving me the greatest childhood ever.

To all the church ladies in the world who still make the best ice cream and will always be there for you when you just can't go it alone.

To all the folks at Ten Speed Press for granting me this amazing opportunity to carry on the *White Trash* series, and with special thanks to Lorena Jones and Julie Bennett. Thank you both for believing in me.

To my newfound extended kin—Tom and Kathryn, Kathy and George, Jeff, Jessica, Ashley, Rick, and Bev. I am so proud to now be part of your family.

To my parents, who have never stopped believing in me, even when I didn't "apply myself" academically. This book is as much yours as it is mine. You both are an inspiration. You give without thought and you love without expectation, and for this I will always be thankful.

And to my husband, Tim, for graciously donating his stomach for a whole year to cornbread and bacon grease. Your undying support and unconditional love will always remain unmatched. You are my best friend, my true ally, and my greatest wish come true.

Introduction

HOT ROLLS AND SWEATY COOKS

I remember how my Granny Boohler's West Virginia kitchen always smelled like hot rolls. Warm and yeasty, the room would bloom with the aroma of fresh baked bread. I'd open the oven door, letting the hot rush of doughy air sweep across my face, waiting to see if the tops had browned, so I could have one roll fresh out. Granny would sneak up behind me and quickly close the door. "You're lettin' all the good air out!" she would cry, and then go back to stirring the sausage gravy so it didn't clump.

Meanwhile, my Aunt Barbara would be laying out the plastic tablecloth—the one with dogwood flowers on it—and topping each place setting with a bright red hand-stitched placemat along with mismatched plates and silverware. Mom would be bustling to and from the basement (where all the "big food" was kept in another fridge) lugging up the country ham, the crispy-skinned turkey, and the giant pot of green beans cooked in fatback. (You know you're a true host when you need two refrigerators to hold all the food you've been cooking.)

As a young girl, my job was always the hors d'oeuvres. Granny would proclaim, "We can't have dinner without hors d'oeuvres!" which I always found funny since most of our dinner "guests" munched on them while wearing dirty sweatpants and wife beaters. I would cube some Colby cheese, get out a few jars of bread-and-butter pickles, throw in a handful of green olives stuffed with pimiento, and then artfully arrange it all in Granny's signature depression glass serving dish. Voila! Hors d'oeuvres.

Now, the "guests" were the men in our family, who avoided the kitchen much in the same way they avoided the washer and dryer and detergent in general. You see, it worked like this. The women cooked the food, served the food, and cleaned up the food while the men ate the food. They had their place—in front of the television, asking for refills of sweet tea and slices of applesauce cake. Simple and highly efficient in a patriarchal sort of way.

In truth, kitchen life for us ladies was easier when we were in total control. Never did I walk into that kitchen and see one of the boys frying up a mess of apple pies draped in one of grandma's aprons proclaiming, "Come and get it!", and never did I want to. We worked much faster as an all-female group. Each of us had her unwritten and unchanging role. My mother and aunt were in charge of cleaning up after Granny, who was well known to leave an apocalyptic mess in her wake. Some nights, it literally rained dirty dishes. They'd be piled up on the kitchen table, the counters, the stoves, in the sink, and even outside on the back porch with all kinds of half-charred, partially congealed vegetable, meat, and fat leavings. It took hours to scrub all those dishes by hand. And the best part was you got to do it all over again the next night. Brittle fingernails and cracked hands were our birthrights.

Granny may have left us with quite a mess, but she sure could cook up a lot of food. From apples to zucchini, she did it all. She'd cook all day every day for a solid week, and everything down to the white bread for leftover turkey sandwiches was made from scratch. One day, she'd make nothing but cakes and pies: coconut, pound, chocolate, chess. Next day would be candies and cookies: turtles, fudge, bourbon balls. Then onto breads: potato rolls, banana bread, zucchini bread. As the grand day of eating approached closer, the turkey, the whole ham, the sweet potato casserole, and the brown beans would be cooked up and stored in the basement fridge with all the other goodies. Finally, the salads would be made: congealed, potato, slaw. The last day would be reserved for gravies, biscuits, punch, and other last-minute doings such as opening fresh jars of blackberry jam, apple butter, and chow chow. This is what country cookin' is all about: flour dusting every biscuit and filling each homemade pie with pure love drawn from the enduring sweat of a hardworking cook.

And Granny's kitchen was small—really small. Imagine a cluster of frenetic women swarming around trying to find space to lay down just one more squash casserole, bumping into one another, knocking over the ice trays laid out for the sweet tea. Imagine all four burners on the cooktop gleaming orange, bubbling over with various gravies and boiling white potatoes. Imagine an oven continuously pumping out black smoke every time you dared to open it (since it hadn't had a real cleaning in years). Imagine no ventilation, no dishwasher, no counter space, and no refrigerator space. Imagine sweating more than you thought you had in you and still making enough food for an entire congregation. Imagine the best time of your life.

Yet, this is how we did it. There was rarely an occasion—we were the occasion. Granny would break out the Fostoria serving platters and the carnival glass, and we always had some kind of green punch served from the antique punchbowl that usually resided in the basement. Gospel music would play from an old 8-track in the adjoining living room, and sometimes Granny would put on a little bluegrass from the tape recorder that rested permanently on the buffet—a little Flatt and Scruggs or her favorite, Mac Wiseman's, "Tis Sweet to Be Remembered."

We didn't have much, but we had a lot, and Granny made sure none of us ever cared about the difference between our family meal and the lobster tails served in some fancy restaurant on real see-through Limoges china. Because this meal, like all of our meals, was special. Granny worked with what she had, and it didn't matter that our forks didn't match or the cole slaw was a little on the sugary side or the punch bowl had a big chip in the rim. This was a feast made from the fortitude of great Southern women treasured by strong, hardworking Southern men. The table was often silent while we ate, not because we were lacking in conversation, but out of respect. A good meal should be savored like a hot roll fresh from the oven and a good host should be cherished, not for what she has, but for what she offers.

☙

This book was written to make my grannies proud. It's a testament to weekly family sit-downs, church socials, mountain-style reunions, and smoky pig pickin's with home-spun, crowd-pleasing recipes straight from West Virginia kitchens. Stories and tall tales are commonplace among these pages and offer a chuckle or two much in the same way they do over a jug of sweet tea at our dinner table. With each story, I've added a few of our favorite family recipes, many of which were rescued from the vaults of my granny's basement—recipes that were scribbled on the backs of napkins, scraps of old newspaper, even directly over the activity page from the Greenview Church bulletin. I found Zurleka's Holiday Cheese Ball (page 66) written on the back of a box of pantyhose.

With this in mind, many of these recipes don't have specific serving yields or amounts, which is just the way my grannies like it. The recipes within this book make simply enough for your crowd, which is around 6 to 8 people, depending on how many hungry eaters you have. Some recipes are simply noted as making a lot—this means that if you are cooking for 6 to 8 people, you will probably be freezing some of the leftovers or saving them for a second-day meal.

My grannies are also very particular regarding the freshness of their ingredients. Growing up on the farm, fresh butter and cream were always in abundance, so store-bought substitutes such as margarine or frozen whipped topping were rarely used. You'll see that many of these recipes call for real butter and freshly whipped cream. This is because we firmly believe that recipes such as the ones you'll find in this book greatly benefit from using the freshest ingredients available, and if that means spending an extra dollar or two on real butter, then so be it.

A few helpful tips and tricks have been added to the end of each section, which should make planning your own gathering a little easier. And no party would be complete without handcrafted centerpieces and decorations, so I've added several crafty ideas like homemade napkin rings made from pinto beans and toilet paper rolls just to give you a smidgin of inspiration.

The book is divided into four sections, with the first three touching on the ways my family does it in West Virginia, with stories, recipes, and tips. From fancy sit-downs, elaborate ice cream socials, and Christmas cooking for a crowd to a simple meal of beans and cornbread fit for a Washington bigwig, I've tried to give readers a taste of how important savoring good food with family and friends is to us. The last section is broken down into recipe categories including salads, meats, vegetables, and desserts, so you can create your own special gathering just the way you like it.

Part One

JUST HAVIN' 'EM OVAH

Chapter 1

SQUIRREL HUNTIN'
AND MISS EDYTHE'S BISCUITS

My daddy used to love squirrel hunting. Next to shooting rats at the local dump on Friday nights with my mother holding the flashlight (a disheartening "date night"), knocking out a few tree rats was the West Virginia pinnacle of entertainment. Back in the 1950s, his favorite weekend getaway consisted of heading down to Deer Creek with his motley group of buddies carrying a mess of shotguns and shooting anything that moved. Hunting would start predawn early, and back then it was not uncommon to ask permission to hunt on private land—a good idea considering that if you didn't you might end up being the one hunted. Much of the law and order in those parts rested in the hands of landowners, good ole boys, and, in rare cases, the local sheriff.

So, my daddy and the boys decided to start the day out hunting the old Clemon's place, where Miss Edythe lived. Miss Edythe, ten years widowed, went to the same local church as most of the town, so daddy figured she would remember him from some past Wednesday night supper or ice cream social and surely give them full permission to hunt her land. But, seeing that Miss Edythe was a bit addled ever since she had that mini stroke a couple of years ago, there was always that slim chance she wouldn't remember a thing.

Yet, up the hill they went, shotguns perched on their shoulders and West Virginia three percent beer hidden in their backpacks. After a few nervous moments (remember, it's not a good idea to venture onto anyone's land you don't know) daddy crept up the rickety porch stairs and knocked his knuckles hard on a swinging screened door riddled with holes and tears. A moment or two passed before a scraggly voice called out, "Who's out there!" followed by the sound of a pair of slippers scraping along a dusty wooden floor.

As the sound of those slippers came closer, the boys eased their way backwards, right back down those creaky, concave wooden stairs. Suddenly, the front door swung open, and the boys shut their eyes tight—they knew they'd be staring down the barrel of Miss Edythe's pistol. And there she was, sure enough as Sunday church, standing on those rickety steps with eyes as big as the New River Gorge. She wore a simple gray dress buttoned tight at the neck that reached all the way down past her ankles, just barely revealing yellowed toenails peeking out from a pair of matted pink slippers. Her hair was white-gray, piled high on her head, and her fire-engine red lipstick smeared up the side of her mouth. She paused a moment to re-tie the string on her gravy-stained apron, and looked up, cocking her head, a bit bewildered at the sight of four scruffy boys standing on her doorstep with loaded shotguns. She stepped back, eyeing them carefully. Then her demeanor began to change. Her face loosened and her eyes suddenly lit up like a brush fire as she hollered, "We'll I'll be damned, you boys finally made it. Y'all git on in here and gitcha somethin' to eat!" And with that, the boys wandered up the front stairs behind her, smiling quietly at their luck.

Country folk love to feed people. Sharing a home-cooked meal is a prerequisite to nearly every activity from union meetings to evening church service to just plain old "visiting." Before any real socializing can take place, you gotta eat and you gotta eat a lot, so as Miss Edythe spoon-dropped more biscuits into the iron skillet, the boys did what any good Southern huntin' boy would do—set down their guns and pulled up a chair.

It was then that Miss Edythe really went to town. Working off a small woodstove, she moved with the efficiency of a seasoned professional chef. She didn't say much while she cooked (like most great chefs), but every once in a while she'd come over to pour out a little more weak brown coffee (so unique to the hills), giving the boys a sideways smile.

Mouths watered as the men patiently watched her toss a large slab of ham tenderloin into the cast iron frying pan. In less than a minute, the expected "shhh" of searing meat filled the small room. You could smell the salt in the air. Next up were the stoneground grits, which went into a big black pot and were covered with just enough water that their little heads couldn't peek out. A little patience and the occasional stir was all they got, since proper grits should be left to their own devices.

Another pan brimmed with Miss Edythe's famous sausage gravy. Anyone who's made a milk-based meat gravy knows that after it sits longer than a few minutes, it can turn into congealed sludge before you can say, "come and get it." She used to say that if you let it sit too long, you might as well spackle the walls with it.

But Miss Edythe knew the secret to bringing that gravy back to life as she grabbed her wooden spoon, poured in a can of milk, and added a generous amount of salt and black pepper. She stirred that gravy 'round and 'round, and soon it was back to its original state—thick, white, creamy, and percolating at a steady simmer. It's these types of culinary nuggets that are whispered under one's breath much in same way a prized recipe is shared in total secrecy. This is cherished information, and if you really want to learn, you'd better watch, and watch close, because what you're witnessing is pure truth in the presence of a woman cooking straight from the heart and straight from the hills.

Soon, like a fine symphony, all of the various musical notes Miss Edythe had created rose to a glorious crescendo played out in boats of sausage gravy, platters of warm biscuits, plates of sliced ham, accented with dabs of homemade butter and dollops of blackberry jam. As the boys mopped up the last bit of gravy with their biscuits, Miss Edythe finally sat down and began to sip her lukewarm coffee. She never ate, but picked a bit at the crumbs left on the near-empty platters. (A true culinary genius cooks to cook, not to eat. I don't think I ever saw my granny sit down and enjoy a full meal in twenty-five years.)

Finally Miss Edythe spoke. She regaled the group with stories of her childhood, great moments of a past foreign to a stuffed-to-the-gills table of young men used to souped-up Chevys, black-and-white television, and indoor plumbing. She told them of the old milkhouse built over Dingess Creek, which runs along her property line, and how she and her late husband, Rodney Dale, built it themselves, splinter by splinter, even cutting the white pines by hand with a hacksaw. She told them how the little "house" was built directly over the cold, flowing mountain water, and how they kept their perishables (milk, cheeses, meats) partially submerged in tin cans so they wouldn't spoil. She recalled her days in the old one-room schoolhouse where during the deep West Virginia winters she would have to wear an extra sweater or two since her desk was positioned away from the glowing heat of the pot-bellied stove.

She laughed as she gossiped about the local church ladies, who, as she said, "were always up in sumbody's bizness." She talked and talked and poured out more coffee as the boys listened with purpose and fascination. But they knew they had to be hitting the road soon, and as they helped Miss Edythe clear the table and put away the dishes, they felt an overwhelming sense of home wash over them. And Daddy, still surprised that Miss Edythe remembered him at all, went over and gave her a big, thank you hug.

"Well, Miss Edythe," he said, "you've really outdone yourself with all this food. This is some of the best cookin' I've had in a long time." The other boys nodded and patted their bellies in enthusiastic agreement. "But, I must say," he added, "I'm real surprised you remembered me from all those years back at Ceres Hollow Church. I was just a little kid back then."

Miss Edythe turned around, gave him a wide, toothy smile, and announced, "Lord honey, I got no idea who you are." And with that, she went back to drying the dishes, although this time, one could've sworn it sounded as if she was barely humming a long forgotten hymn from the old church back in Ceres Hollow. "O may we meet and be complete, and long together dwell, and serve the Lord with one accord, and so, dear friends, farewell."

☙

COUSIN EUGENE'S COUNTRY CORNCAKES

Corncakes are a staple in any country kitchen, but in order to do 'em right, you need to add real meat drippings. In our house, we always kept a little jar of congealed drippings next to the stove. Every time we fried up some bacon, pork, or country sausage, we'd pour out the leftover grease into that little jar. When it was time to cook up our cakes, we'd scoop out a tablespoon or two of drippings into a hot griddle and fry up our cakes until they were nice and golden brown.

3 to 4 tablespoons sausage,
  bacon, country ham, or
  pork chop drippings
1 cup white stoneground cornmeal
$1/2$ cup golden yellow self-rising
  cornbread mix
1 level teaspoon sugar

$1/3$ teaspoon salt
Pinch of baking soda
1 tablespoon baking powder
1 egg
1 cup buttermilk
Butter for serving

Get your cast iron griddle real hot.

Put about 2 tablespoons of the drippings in your griddle. Spread the grease evenly around with a paper towel. The drippings will be just shy of "smoking" when ready for the corncake batter. (Add extra drippings as needed.)

Sift up your cornmeal, cornbread mix, sugar, salt, baking soda, and baking powder in a big bowl. Whisk your egg in a little bowl and then add in the buttermilk. Pour your egg and buttermilk mixture into your dry ingredients. Stir until the batter is well mixed and about the consistency of pancake batter.

Cook up your cakes until the downside is golden and crusty. Give your cakes a flip and cook a little more. Spread the hot cakes with a slab of butter and serve them right from the pan.

Who's a Comin'?

My grandpa just couldn't stand a crowded house, so if we ever had enough guests to create a line to the bathroom, it was time to rent out a pavilion at the 4-H club.

Miss Edythe may not remember invitin' ya, but when you're craftin' up your own party, make sure you've got the right folks comin' to your gathering. We always invite family and friends, and we never forget the folks we see on a regular basis like our pastor, hairdresser, bank tellers, and grocery check-out gals. And we never forget to invite the sheriff, especially if we're having a barbecue, because you never know when things might get rowdy.

Make sure you mention specific attire on your handmade invites, unless you want your guests to arrive in sweatpants, dirty undershirts, and acid wash jeans.

BYOB stands for "Bring your own box of wine," "Bring your own banjo," "Bring your own beer huggy," or "Bring your own Billy Bob teeth."

It was always more special to hand-draw a birthday card than buy one, so I try to do the same when making invites. We've made them from cut-out pieces of cardboard, burlap sacks, and even square-cut pieces of leftover grocery bags. Decorate your invites with family portraits or a big gelatin concoction for added flavor.

DINGESS CREEK HAM AND RED-EYE GRAVY

Get your cast iron skillet real hot. Add a little shortening, and let it melt. Then toss in a big slab of country ham. Cook your ham good on both sides and then take it out and put it on a plate. Turn up your skillet a bit and add about a $1/2$ cup of strong coffee. Be sure to stir in the little ham crispies off the bottom of the pan. Then pour your coffee gravy over your ham and serve it up with a pile of Miss Edythe's Old Fashion' Buttermilk Biscuits (page 8).

NORMA LOU'S APPLE BUTTER

Apple butter is a staple in every West Virginia kitchen. A popular fruit butter, apple butter is made from the pulp of ripe, red apples, cooked down and strained into sterilized jars. Just make sure to always use red apples. My great aunt, Norma Lou, once made a batch with green apples and brought it to a church picnic. That was the last time she did that! Her ugly, pale green apple butter was the talk of the town because everyone knows you never use green apples to make real apple butter.

5 cups apple cider
10 pounds tart red cooking apples, washed, cored, and cut into wedges
4 to 5 cups sugar

$1^1/2$ teaspoons ground cinnamon, or more if you want it
1 box red cinnamon candies (50 to 60 candies)

Get out your heavy-bottomed pan and bring the cider to a boil. Cook it down to $2^1/2$ cups. Add in your apples and simmer until they are mushy but no longer watery. Expect this to take a couple of hours. Push your apple mixture through a sieve or colander to remove skin and lumps. Now, measure out your pulp mixture and put it back in your pot. Add between $1/2$ and 1 cup of sugar per cup of pulp depending on how sweet you like it. Add the cinnamon and cinnamon candies. Cook, covered, on medium-high heat for 6 to 8 hours, or until your mixture gets nice and thick and will hold its shape. Give it a stir every now and then so it doesn't stick.

At this point, you can add more cinnamon if you want, or more sugar. Pack the apple butter, which should be a dark reddish brown, into hot sterilized pint canning jars, leaving $1/4$ inch headspace. Seal your jars while the mixture is still piping hot. Apple butter is delicious spread on homemade biscuits and breads. Properly sealed apple butter can be stored in a cool, dark place for up to two years.

MISS EDYTHE'S OLD FASHION' BUTTERMILK BISCUITS

If you're from the South, you live by one solid truth—it just ain't a meal without a pile of fresh, hot homemade biscuits. While there are many variations—mayonnaise biscuits, cornmeal biscuits, angel biscuits—it's the buttermilk biscuit that sets the standard. Whether you're using store-bought buttermilk or your own homemade sour milk, it's that all-familiar tang hitting your tongue with each bite that makes these biscuits the absolute best.

2 cups flour, sifted	$^3/_4$ teaspoon salt
2 teaspoons baking powder	$^1/_4$ cup shortening
$^1/_4$ teaspoon baking soda	1 cup buttermilk

Turn on your oven to 475 degrees.

Sift up your dry ingredients in a bowl. Cut in the shortening with a couple of dinner knives. Stir in your buttermilk until you have yourself a soft dough. Knead the dough on a floured surface until it's smooth, and cut your biscuits with an open, clean tin can. Put the biscuits on a lightly greased-up baking sheet and bake for 10 to 12 minutes, or until lightly browned on top. Serve 'em up hot.

JOYCIE FRAZIER'S BUTTERMILK PIE

Southerners love their buttermilk. My Grandpa Woody used to drink a big glass of it with his dinner, and my daddy still loves to eat it mixed with day-old cornbread for dessert (see page 27). We make biscuits, muffins, gravies, cakes, and even pies with the stuff, and as you'll see with this classic super-sweet, rich pie, this is as straightforward as it gets.

$1^1/_2$ sticks butter	3 eggs
2 cups sugar	1 cup buttermilk
3 tablespoons flour	2 unbaked 8-inch pie shells

Turn on your oven to 300 degrees.

Cream up your butter and sugar together real good. Add the rest of your ingredients. Mix and pour into 2 unbaked pie shells.

Bake for 1 to 1¹/₂ hours, or until set. Cool on a wire rack.

DOWN AT THE MILKHOUSE BREAKFAST CASSEROLE

This is a great way to entertain your overnight guests without having to cook all morning long. Make this self-contained breakfast a day ahead and stick it in the fridge overnight. All you have to do in the morning is put on a pot of coffee and set a while with your guests while your casserole bakes.

1 pound ground breakfast sausage
4 tablespoons butter
6 slices white bread
12 eggs
³/₄ cup milk
1 can cream of mushroom soup
Salt and pepper, as much as you like

3 to 4 green onions, minced
2 tablespoons chopped fresh parsley, or 1 teaspoon dried
Dash of hot sauce (or more if your guests like it spicy)
1¹/₂ cups grated sharp Cheddar cheese

Brown up your sausage in a medium skillet. Spread the butter over the bottom and sides of a casserole dish. Then put your bread pieces on the bottom of it. Get yourself another bowl and beat up your eggs, milk, and soup, and add salt and pepper the way you like it. Add in the onions, parsley, and hot sauce. Pour this mixture over your bread. Top with the cooked sausage and then cover the whole mess with a bunch of cheese. Now, cover the dish and stick it in your fridge overnight.

Next morning, turn on your oven to 350 degrees. Bring your casserole close to room temperature before puttin' it in a hot oven (or you might just crack your casserole dish). Bake uncovered for about 30 to 35 minutes. Serve up hot.

CERES HOLLER BAKED CHEESE GRITS

Don't be a grit hater. We need to save the grit haters from themselves. Grit haters knock this tasty corn by-product because they've been eating over-processed, finely ground corn that merely mimics the real stuff. They've been wasting their tastebuds on that bland, runny mush far too long. Serve this recipe to even your meanest grit hater and I can bet you'll win 'em over with the first bite.

6 cups chicken stock, plus more
   as needed for consistency
2 cups milk or heavy cream
1^1/$_4$ cups stoneground grits
1 stick butter, cut into pieces
1^1/$_2$ cups grated sharp Cheddar cheese
   (use more if you like 'em cheesy)

4 to 5 green onions, chopped
Couple of dashes of hot sauce
Salt and pepper, as much as you like
3 eggs, beaten

Turn on your oven to 350 degrees.

Get out a deep cast iron pot. Bring up your chicken stock and milk to a slow boil (start out with 2 cups of the stock and hold on to the rest for adding later if grits are too thick). Whisk in your grits. Cook grits, uncovered, on low heat until they lose their "crunch," adding more chicken stock and stirring as necessary. Be careful to stir the grits as often as possible so they don't clump and stick to the bottom of your pan. It'll take a while, so set back and catch up on some local gossip while you stir.

Once your grits are cooked, take 'em off the heat and add your butter, some of the cheese (save some to sprinkle on top), the green onions, hot sauce, and salt and pepper. Cool your mixture a bit and then whisk in your eggs. Grease up a casserole dish and pour in the grits mixture. Bake for about 30 to 40 minutes, or until lightly golden and puffy.

VIOLA'S COCONUTTY BLACK WALNUT CAKE

My Granny (a.k.a. Viola) and Granddaddy Belcher had a couple of huge towering black walnut trees in their backyard up in Bluefield, West Virginia. It wasn't uncommon to see those deliciously pungent walnuts turn up in just about everything she baked, from sweet buns to turkey dressing to this absolutely delicious pound cake topped with a warm, homemade coconut syrup. This is one of many cakes Granny Belcher loved to serve up at the crack of dawn with a hot mug of Postum. Our "real" breakfast, complete with bacon, eggs, and biscuits, was usually served several hours later.

2 cups sugar	1 cup chopped black walnuts
1 cup vegetable oil	1 cup sweetened flaked coconut
4 eggs, beaten	2 teaspoons coconut extract
3 cups all-purpose flour	
$1/2$ teaspoon salt	1 cup sugar
$1/2$ teaspoon baking soda	$1/2$ cup water
$1/2$ teaspoon baking powder	2 tablespoons butter
1 cup buttermilk	1 teaspoon coconut extract

Turn on your oven to 325 degrees. Grease up and flour a 10-inch bundt cake (tube) pan.

Combine together your sugar, oil, and eggs. Beat it all real good. Next, mix up your dry ingredients in another bowl and then add it to the sugar mixture, alternating with buttermilk and beating well after you add it. Next, stir in your nuts, coconut, and coconut extract. Pour batter into your prepared pan and bake for about 1 hour, or until a toothpick stuck in the center of the cake comes out clean.

To mix up the syrup for pouring over the cake, put your sugar, water, and butter in a small saucepan. Bring it all to a boil, then lower the heat and cook for 5 minutes. Remove from heat and stir in the extract. Reheat until very warm before pouring over cake.

Keep your cake in the pan for at least 4 hours before cuttin' into it! Pour the syrup over the cake after it is removed from the pan.

Dried Beef Jar Juice Glasses

Next time you whip up a mess of Blasphemin' on a Shingle (page 57) don't throw out your dried beef jars. Save 'em, and before you know it, you'll have a whole set of juice glasses, which just might come in handy if you find yourself with unexpected guests for breakfast.

You can also take your glasses and use 'em to can jelly with a paraffin seal, fill 'em up with fruit wine at dinner, or line 'em up on a nearby fencepost and start shootin'.

Chapter 2

WE CAN'T HAVE DINNER
WITHOUT HORS DE VOOS

I don't remember a single family gatherin' at my Granny Boohler's West Virginia rancher without a selection of proper, mountain-style hors d'oeuvres. There was, of course, the relish plate, brimming with homemade bread-and-butter pickles, pimiento-stuffed olives, and baby dills properly displayed in a three-sectioned serving dish complete with a half bent-up tarnished silver appetizer fork.

Granny's table was always decorated with the finest linens she had, most of which had been given to her over the years as handmade gifts from friends and neighbors. The placemats were hand stitched with red Cardinals or Golden Delicious apples or "Jesus Loves You" sewn in big black script letters. Granny wasn't exactly known for keeping her things too organized, so it was a rare occasion that any of the linens actually matched one another, therefore making the table a veritable smorgasboard of color and country-fried originality. "Jesus Loves You" would be set next to the giant Cardinal, which would be set next to a plastic mat with a rooster caught in midtrot, which would be set next to the Golden Delicious placemat. Throw in a couple of dried beef candle holders (see page 18), a centerpiece fashioned out of handmade paper flowers (see page 54), and an oversized punch bowl filled with alcohol-free, red-tinted juice, and you have the commencement of Granny's hors de voos hour.

Various nibbles such as cheese balls, dips, and crackers, as well as more substantial fare like grape jelly meatballs, fried oysters, and pepperoni rolls, would be laid out in steaming crockpots and hairline-cracked serving platters. These goodies were a meal in and of themselves, and considering we had just eaten the breakfast to end all breakfasts a mere two to three hours earlier, the thought of this buffet spread acting as a preface to the "real" dinner was enough to make one's stomach churn in disbelief. But like all good country people who never turn down hearty home-cooked food, we loaded up our paper plates anyway, content in the thought that we were still wearing our West Virginia University sweatpants with the stretchy, elastic waistbands.

Meatballs were then lanced with wooden toothpicks while the cornmeal fried oysters (a precious and rare commodity in our house) were literally fought over by hand. The pepperoni rolls oozed melted mozzarella with each bite, which always created an awkward beverage pairing with the fire engine red, overly sweet punch. As we ate, the cheese ball slowly diminished, and as usual, the serving knife was dismissed in favor of shoving crackers directly into the spread.

But there was one fundamental irony to be found in all of this family camaraderie. We gathered around the table, and we ate the food, but we never really interacted. Anyone who has entertained knows that the purpose of serving hors de voos is to have your guests linger by the food, chatting, sharing stories, and generally facilitating some sort of human contact, above and beyond grunting and burping. Instead, the men in the family would spend the day in front of the television, usually watching "the game," and once the women had decorated, cooked, and laid out all the tasty goodies, the men would come in, load up a plate, scoop out some punch (skipping the ladle and using the cup), return to the living room and to their same spot on the couch, and proceed to eat in silence. The philosophy was this: load it up, stuff it in, and sit on it until more food appears.

But Granny never cared. Why? Because grannies love to feed people. For many grannies, it's less about cooking the food and more about watching you eat the food. Conversation is secondary to watching you ooh, aah, and groan in repeated moments of food-induced ecstasy. The fact that your orgasmic rumblings take place in front of the television with a tray of food in your lap will be conveniently overlooked. So, the next time you head to your granny's house and there is more food laid out than a competitive eater could consume and it's not even dinner yet, you'd better eat, and you'd better eat good. Unhook that belt and take a deep breath. Forget the diet, forget your lactose intolerance, forget that you just ate less than an hour ago. This is granny time, and you better deliver.

જી

OYSTER CRISPIES

Save your cornmeal mixture and your oyster liquor from making Stringbean Earl's Cornmeal-Fried Oysters (facing page). Pour your liquor into the cornmeal mixture. Add a little minced onion and enough sweet milk or buttermilk to make a batter that is a little thicker than pancake batter. Drop by spoonfuls into hot oil and fry up until golden brown. Drain on paper towels. Serve 'em up hot along with the fried oysters!

STRINGBEAN EARL'S
CORNMEAL-FRIED OYSTERS

1 quart fresh oysters

1 cup cornmeal

1 cup instant cornbread mix

Salt and pepper, as much as you like

Shortening, for frying

Get your oysters as close to room temperature as you can, letting them sit in the liquor they come in.

Heat up your cast iron skillet and add enough shortening for a shallow fry (about 1 inch to 1½ inches of melted oil). Mix the cornmeal and cornbread mix together in a wide, shallow bowl. Add salt and pepper the way you like it. Take your oysters out of their liquid, reserving that liquid to make Oyster Crispies (facing page), and roll real good in the cornmeal mix. Fry in the hot oil and drain on paper towels. Sprinkle your oysters with a little salt as soon as they come out of the pan. Serve 'em hot.

CLEAN LIVIN' BAPTIST PUNCH

You gotta break out the punch bowl for this delicious, alcohol-free punch because it's a real showstopper. Float plastic flowers on top for added decadence.

2 packages cherry or strawberry
  Kool Aid

1 large (12-ounce) can frozen
  orange juice

2 quarts water

1 large (64-ounce) can pineapple
  juice, cold

1½ cups sugar, or to taste

1½ liter bottles of ginger ale, cold

1 pint sherbert (vanilla, orange, pineapple,
  or your favorite)

Get out your punch bowl and add in your Kool Aid mix, orange juice, water, pineapple juice, and sugar. Mix it up real good. Pour in your ginger ale and spoon in your sherbert.

Tablescapin' and Decoratin'

Bust out that punch bowl! Homemade punch, like Clean Livin' Baptist Punch (page 15), is a must if you want to do it Granny style. Choose your flavor, but plan on dumping a pile of green or orange sherbert in at some point 'cuz that's what makes it extra good. Speaking of punch, just in case you might have some God-fearin' Southern Baptists at your table, leave out the booze (unless, of course, you sneak it in).

Don't forget to hand out hand-stitched pillows for your guests to sit on. Some favorite sayings stitched onto pillows in our house were "If momma ain't happy, ain't nobody happy" and "Never trust a skinny cook." You might like to add these or other phrases to your napkins or placemats as well.

Our placemats and glassware rarely matched since much of it ended up lost or broken over the years, but that never stopped Granny from using them. Even her most cherished carnival glass, which was often missing pieces and visibly chipped, was pulled out every time we sat down to eat, whether we were having a simple meal of sandwiches and milk or a full-fledged turkey dinner. Granny was never afraid to get fancy, and you shouldn't be either. For us that often meant breaking out the unpolished silverware and servingware, most of which remained unused throughout the meal since eating with one's hands also had its place.

I don't ever remember having real flowers at Granny's table. We always had paper or plastic ones since florists weren't the easiest thing to come by in the hills. Granny had a collection of colorful plastic flowers in the attic and she would crawl up the pull-down stairs to gather what she needed for the evening's centerpiece. They never needed water, only a slight dusting here and there.

MISS CYNDI'S WHITE TRASH SUSHI

The thought of eating raw fish wrapped up in seaweed would certainly send my granny a prayin', but wrap up a dill pickle in white bread and cream cheese and she'll be singing "How Great Thou Art" in no time. This nifty little appetizer is a great one to take to your next gatherin' just to show everyone how much you appreciate other cultures.

White bread
1 (8-ounce) block of cream cheese
Baby or midget dill pickles

Cut the crusts off your white bread. Cover the bread with a thick layer of cream cheese. The more, the better. Lay a pickle on the bread. Roll the bread around the pickle (just like sushi) and seal the edges (just smush 'em together). Cut into $3/4$-inch slices and serve.

ALL DRESSED UP CHEESE BALL

Every family gatherin' needs a fancy cheese ball. This little ball of goodness is made up of cream cheese, pineapple, green pepper, and pecans, and is a surefire hit at any party. Serve with Ritz crackers or homemade toast points if you really want to impress your guests.

1 (8-ounce) package cream cheese, softened
$1/3$ cup canned crushed pineapple, drained
$1/3$ cup minced green pepper
1 green onion, including the tops, minced

$1/2$ cup toasted pecans, chopped, plus some untoasted pecan halves for decorating
Salt and pepper, as much as you like
Pinch of cayenne pepper

Mix up all of your ingredients in the order listed and stir up real good. Roll into a fancy ball, cover in plastic, and chill in your refrigerator overnight. Decorate your ball with extra pecans halves if you want.

Dried Beef Jar Candle Holders

What better place to put those tea lights than in a dressed-up dried beef jar? Just wash out your jars real good, paint 'em up (or stencil them) the way you like it, then stick a tea light in each one to decorate your table. No one will ever know your tea light holder was once a Sunday night supper.

MISS OMA'S GRAPE JELLY MEATBALLS

$1^{1}/_{2}$ cups Burney Papper's
   Chili Sauce (facing page)
$^{1}/_{2}$ medium-sized jar grape jelly
   (or more if you like it sweet!)
1 pound ground beef
2 tablespoons breadcrumbs

1 egg
$^{1}/_{3}$ cup chopped onion
$^{1}/_{2}$ tablespoon prepared horseradish
1 clove garlic, minced
Salt and pepper, as much as you like

Put the chili sauce and grape jelly in a crockpot set on medium-low heat.

For your meatballs, mix together the ground beef with the rest of the ingredients. Carefully shape the mixture into small balls, taking care not to roll the meatballs too tightly.

Fry the meatballs in a shallow pan of hot oil until they're brown on all sides. Add them to the grape jelly mixture and simmer until nice and tender. Serve straight from the pot with toothpicks.

MOM'S WEST VIRGINIA PEPPERONI ROLLS

Some call the pepperoni roll the state food of West Virginia. Created by Italian immigrant coal miners as an easy-to-eat handheld lunch while on the job, the pepperoni roll has achieved iconic status. Consisting of a couple strips of spicy pepperoni enrobed in a warm, slightly sweet dough, this portable treat has many variations. Here is my family's version, which is topped with peppers canned in a spicy tomato sauce and melted mozzarella.

4 large submarine rolls
1 stick pepperoni, peeled and
   cut into thin slices

Shredded mozzarella cheese
1 (15-ounce) jar canned
   peppers in tomato sauce

Turn on your oven to 350 degrees. Grease up a baking sheet.

Slice open the rolls and layer the pepperoni on the bottom. Sprinkle on 1 layer of shredded cheese, 1 layer of peppers in tomato sauce, and top with another lighter layer of cheese. Wrap loosely in tin foil (so the top of the roll is fully exposed). Put the rolls in the oven for about 8 to 10 minutes, or until the cheese is fully melted. Serve hot.

Burney Papper's Chili Sauce

We just love making our own sauces, relishes, and spreads. From homemade ketchup to hotdog chili to chow chow relish, we make 'em all. Burney Papper's is a slang term for hot peppers. For Miss Oma's Grape Jelly Meatballs (facing page), use this homemade chili sauce instead of store-bought.

$1^1/_2$ cups white vinegar
$1^1/_2$ cups brown sugar
1 tablespoon salt, plus more as needed
9 cups chopped tomatoes

$1^1/_2$ cups chopped onion
2 whole jalapenos, sliced in half
1 whole cinnamon stick and 1 teaspoon
   whole cloves, tied up in cheesecloth

Get your vinegar, brown sugar, and salt to boiling in a good-sized pot. Add your tomatoes, onions, and peppers. Add the tied-up spices. Cook, uncovered, on low heat until thickened (about $1^1/_2$ hours), stirrin' every now and then. Skim off your foam from time to time. For a thinner sauce, cool and purée in a blender. Store in pint jars.

Chapter 3

BEANS, CORNBREAD, AND POLITICKIN'

As often as my Granny Boohler entertained, it came as no surprise when one afternoon she sat me down with two, big sweet iced teas to tell me the story of our family's greatest claim to culinary fame—the time she cooked a full-on beans and cornbread dinner for her most prominent dinner guest, our very own "West Virginian of the Twentieth Century," U.S. Senator Robert C. Byrd.

Back in the early to mid-1970s, both my granny and grandpa were rather active in local politics. As a public health nurse at the local hospital, Granny was often involved in issues related to health care and education. One of her biggest concerns, and a legitimate one at that, was the quality of health care (or, rather, lack thereof) that families living in more rural areas of the state were receiving. For many, a trip to the doctor for a check-up could result in literally hours of travel. Like others involved in the cause, Granny believed that implementing rural medical outreach programs, including bringing in more doctors, nurses, and other medical personnel to the hills, was desperately needed. And there was one very important person who happened to agree with her—Senator Robert Byrd.

Not ones to pass up a chance to politicize, Granny and Grandpa attended a meeting at the local church where Senator Byrd was speaking on issues related to improving health care. When the meeting was over, they went up to wish him well, and then straight outta the blue asked the senator to join them for dinner. It may seem shocking that they didn't think twice about asking him over, but that's how country people do it. It's not about how famous you are, it's about how hungry you are.

Now, the senator is a well-known beans and cornbread lover. Like many West Virginians during the depression, he was raised in a small coal town, coincidentally not far from where my grandfather and great-grandfather worked as miners. His story is one of achieving great success in the face of considerable odds, and although Senator Byrd may reside in Washington, his heart still rests in a little house up the holler. And apparently, so does his stomach.

It seems that the older we get, the more we want to go back to that one meal that tastes like home. For mountain folk, it's the beans and cornbread meal. Pinto beans simmered all day with a slug of fatback served alongside a big wedge of savory cornbread. Throw in a little chow chow (our version of relish), some chopped green onions, and a dollop of ketchup and you've got true peasant food at its finest.

When Granny went to work in her little kitchen on that snowy afternoon, she knew exactly what the senator wanted to eat, and she was a true master at making it. Just the day before she had whipped up a big pot of brown beans, so she set to work on some cornbread (we call it "grit bread") baked in a cast iron skillet. To go alongside, apples from her backyard were gathered from the root cellar, sliced, and fried up in leftover bacon grease.

It wasn't long before Senator Byrd and his entourage arrived, took off their snow-dusted coats, and sat down to a table brimming with West Virginia specialties. After Grandpa gave the blessing (he always did this, as head of the household), the group began to eat, but not before Senator Byrd said his quick prayer of thanks. And then, like any proper country boy, he stuck his napkin into his shirt before spooning one single bite of beans into his mouth. They ate and ate, and talked about family, growing up in the coalfields, local politics, and God. Sweet tea was poured in abundance, and seconds were served more than once. Granny proudly watched it all happen, knowing deep in her heart that she was always built to cook for kings and queens. After all, the senator exclaimed more than once that he hadn't had cooking this good since he ate at Lady Bird's.

After dessert, the senator mentioned that he had a nationally televised speaking engagement later that evening and would they mind if he rested a while before taking off, especially after eating all that good food. So again, like a true West Virginia hostess, Granny didn't think twice. She escorted the senator to the basement rec room that Grandpa built himself, fluffed him a pillow, and draped a warm blanket over his shoulders. In a matter of moments, he was on his back fast asleep, with his black sock–clad feet barely poking out from under the blanket. To Granny, he was just another hardworking man from the coalfields, who, in this particular repose, seemed more like the young man who spent time working as a meat cutter and who loved to play the fiddle than a big-city politician who was twice elected president pro tempore, making him third in line for the presidency of the United States. She leaned over to cover his feet and let out a short giggle when she saw that one of his socks had a hole in it the size of a quarter.

After an hour or so, the senator awakened, fully refreshed. Granny and Grandpa said their farewells, and as the senator put on his coat, Granny straightened his tie. It was then she saw it—a big bean stain right on the top part of his polka-dot tie. "Mr. Senator," she said. "I'm afraid you're going to have to take off your tie. Seems you've got a bit of a spot on it." The senator looked down to see the offensive stain and quickly removed his tie. "Don't think I can go on television with this old thing!" he joked as he removed it and handed it over to Granny.

"Here. Let me," Grandpa said, as he took off his own tie and handed it to the senator. "It would be an honor if you wore mine." And with that, the senator said his thanks, put on his new tie, and left to greet his public.

Later that evening, as my Granny and Grandpa reminisced about how good her beans were and how funny it was that their senator had holes in his socks, they turned on the television to watch his public address. There he was, a standing proud West Virginian, bathed in lights and fanfare that only politics can bring, and wearing my grandpa's tie. In that moment, the lines that separate poverty from excess, backwoods from Park Avenue, and insignificant coal towns from a parking spot at the U.S. Capitol were blurred, if only for one snowy day.

❧

BACON GREASE FRIED APPLES

Fry enough bacon for breakfast and save the grease. Cut up enough tart cooking apples (peels on) for your crowd. In a cast iron or heavy-bottomed pan, heat a couple of tablespoons of bacon grease. Throw in your apples and cook 'em on medium-low heat. Add a little sugar and keep on cooking. You know they're done when the apples are mushy and the sugar has caramelized.

THE SENATOR'S BROWN BEANS AND FATBACK

This bean recipe is truly fit for kings and queens. Serve it up with a wedge of cornbread, homemade chow chow (below), and minced sweet onions for a taste of true peasant food. Just make sure to remove your tie before diggin' in since this dish makes for messy eatin'. But beware, brown beans and fatback can be addictive, and as of yet, there is no known cure except more brown beans and fatback.

1 (16-ounce) package dried pinto beans
1 medium to large slug of salt fatback, or 1 to 2 meaty pork ribs
$1^1/_2$ quarts water
Salt and pepper, as much as you like

Put your beans and water in a cooking pot on medium heat. Next, stick your fatback in a microwavable coffee cup and cover with water. Microwave on high for 30 seconds or so, then turn the fat over and do the same for another 30 seconds. Pour the fatback and broth into the cooking beans. Once the beans begin to lightly boil at medium heat, lower the temperature to low and cook for 2 hours, or until they're soft like you like 'em.

JEB MAGRUDER'S CHOW CHOW

2 cups chopped red bell peppers	4 cups chopped cored green tomatoes
2 cups chopped green bell peppers	3 tablespoons pickling salt
4 cups chopped cabbage	4 tablespoons mustard seed
2 cups chopped sweet onions	2 tablespoons celery seed
2 hot banana peppers, chopped	1 cup sugar
5 cucumbers, chopped	2 cups cider vinegar

Sprinkle your vegetables with pickling salt; cover and refrigerate overnight. Lightly rinse your veggies and drain 'em well.

Put the rest of the ingredients in a large pot, and bring to a boil. Add the vegetable mixture and cook for about 10 minutes. Pack into sterilized canning jars, leaving about $1/_2$ inch headspace. Remove any air bubbles. Wipe jar rims and seal at once according to canning manufacturer's directions. This recipe makes about 8 pints.

K.G.'S COUNTRY GRIT BREAD

Grit bread is similar to cornbread, but it's made with pure stoneground grits, giving it a unique texture unlike any you've ever tasted. This bread is dense and moist on the inside while golden and crusty on the outside.

1 cup plain white stoneground cornmeal (not instant)	1/3 teaspoon baking soda
3/4 cup yellow self-rising cornbread mix	3 to 4 tablespoons sausage, bacon, country ham, or pork chop drippings
1 teaspoon sugar	1/4 cup plain white stoneground grits
1/2 teaspoon salt	3/4 cup water
1 tablespoon baking powder	1 egg
	1 cup buttermilk

Turn on your oven to 475 degrees.

Sift up your white cornmeal, yellow self-rising cornbread mix, sugar, salt, baking powder, and baking soda into a big mixing bowl.

Put your fat drippings in a cast iron cornbread pan (or muffin or cornstick pan) and warm them on the stove. When your drippings are melted, tilt your pan so the sides and bottom are well greased up.

Mix up your grits and water in a bowl and cook in your microwave on high for 3 minutes. Stop and stir and then microwave again on high for 3 minutes and set aside. The grits will be about half done, but that's okay.

Whisk your egg in a bowl. Then add your egg with your buttermilk to the dry ingredients. Stir until the batter is well mixed but still a bit on the firm and dry side. Now add the extra pan drippings and your grits. Mix all of the ingredients good with a large spoon. (If grits and water have cooled, reheat for 30 seconds before adding.) Your batter shouldn't be too dry or too wet, but somewhere in between.

Pour batter into your cornbread pan and bake for 20 to 25 minutes. (Cornsticks take slightly less time.) Your Grit Bread is done when a nice golden brown crust has formed. Now, all you need to do is get a big slab of butter and dig in!

Cooking Tip:

Leftover grit bread makes mouthwatering fried cornbread. For fried bread, slice cornbread into pie-shaped wedges and then slice each into 2 half wedges, each with a soft side and a crusty side. Next, heat your griddle or fry pan to medium-hot and drop in a small piece of butter. Place one of your half wedges (soft side down) on the sizzling hot butter. Do the same for the rest of your half wedges. Cook until a golden brown. Finally, lower your heat to warm and turn all the half wedges over. Allow the other side to heat thoroughly and eat 'em while they're hot.

CIDER VINEGAR KURLY KALE

The best part of eatin' a mess of kurly kale is drinking the leftover pot likker (page 28) left at the bottom of your pot, so make sure you don't throw it out.

1 to 1¹/₂ pounds kurly kale
1 medium slug of salt fatback, or 1 to 2 meaty pork ribs
    (smoked turkey necks work good, too)
2 cups water
Salt to taste (less needed with salt fatback)
Apple cider vinegar, for serving

Get yourself a big pot. Put a little water in your pot and add your fatback or pork ribs. Put a lid on and cook for about a half hour on medium-low.

In the meantime, wash your kurly kale really good and cut into bite-sized pieces. Throw your kale into your water mixture after the fatback has cooked for a good half hour and put your lid back on. Let it go for about another hour, longer if you like your kale real tender. Salt and pepper the way you like it.

Serve your kale with a splash of cider vinegar.

Meetin', Greetin', and Sittin' at the Table

Set the stage. Turn off the television, let the dogs out, make up a big batch of sweet tea, and sweep the dust bunnies under the living room carpet.

If you've got holes in your socks, don't take your shoes off.

Know your beans. Be up to date on current events, such as upcoming races at your local speedway, the first day of huntin' season, and who Widow Shifflet had over for dinner last night.

Keep feeding people 'til they can no longer function and must have a nap. Prepare a quiet area of the house for this purpose, complete with blankets and pillows.

Set the tone by tucking your napkin directly into your shirt. Feel free to use your fingers to eat any food that spills onto your napkin. (Note: A well-tucked napkin can help prevent any tie spillage but is not guaranteed.)

MY GRANDDADDY'S CORNBREAD AND MILK

I remember the first time I saw my granddaddy having a glass of cornbread and milk. I was about eight years old, and like any kid, I was always looking for something sweet to eat. One night after dinner, I glanced down at the end of the table where he always sat and watched him drink this frothy glass of yellow mush. It looked like a vanilla shake but was much thicker and chunky. Every time he sipped it, his neck would go limp and his eyes would roll back up into his head as if he were having some kind of buttermilk-induced blackout.

After much pestering, he finally gave me a taste. It was a little sweet, a little mushy, a little tangy, and plenty thick. I had never tasted anything of its kind. "You like it?" he asked. I couldn't admit that I didn't. But I wanted him to think I absolutely loved it, so I nodded in appreciation. "Well, here's some more," he said, as he spooned more cornbread into my buttermilk-soaked glass.

After that I had cornbread and milk after dinner, as a snack, as a side dish, and as my breakfast, and I sat right next to my granddaddy every time. His eyes would roll back up into his head in a moment of bliss as he took the first swallow while mine would tear up as I choked the stuff down. But I'd smile and he'd smile, and that made it all worthwhile.

My granddaddy passed away a couple of years ago, and as I read his eulogy to family and friends down at the Greenview Methodist Church, I couldn't help but recall his great appreciation for simple food, from the way he had to have those green beans cooked down to nothing to how he overslathered his rolls in butter. But it was how he cherished the most simple meal on earth, a huge swig of buttermilk filled with hand-torn chunks of cornbread, that made him who he was—a hardworking man who, at the end of a long day, found his own paradise at the bottom of a glass.

Leftover cornbread
Big glass of sweet milk or buttermilk

Fill your glass about three-quarters of the way full with the leftover cornbread. Mash it down some or simply crumble it with your hands. Pour your milk over the top and drink straight from the glass, or grab yourself a spoon and dig in.

PINTO BEAN PIE

It's official. We country folk will literally make anything out of pinto beans. This pie tastes very similar to pumpkin pie and gets even better when your guests don't quite know what they're eating. Serve with a side of Beano.

$1^1/_2$ cups dried pinto beans

3 medium or 2 extra large eggs, beaten

$^1/_2$ cup white sugar

$^1/_2$ cup brown sugar

1 (13-ounce) can evaporated milk

$^1/_2$ stick butter, melted

1 teaspoon ground cloves

$1^1/_2$ teaspoons ground cinnamon

$^1/_2$ teaspoon salt

Whipped cream for serving

Cook up your beans in plain ole water until real tender, about 3 hours at a low simmer. Strain, and reserve $^1/_2$ cup of the cooking liquid.

Turn on your oven to 450 degrees.

Get out your blender and purée your beans with the $^1/_2$ cup of bean cooking liquid. Your mixture should look like thin mashed potatoes. Add the rest of your ingredients and mix real good. Pour your bean filling into a 9-inch pie shell and bake for about 15 minutes. Turn down your oven temperature to 350 degrees and cook your pie for another 45 to 55 minutes, or until it sets up. Serve warm with whipped cream.

Pot Likker Spring Tonic

The broth, or pot likker as we like to call it, at the bottom of a pot of cooked greens is loaded with nutrients and makes an excellent dipping sauce for a wedge of cornbread. It also makes a healthy spring tonic. Just pour out any leftover pot likker into a juice glass and drink it down. It'll cure what ails ya!

Pinto Bean Toilet Paper Roll Napkin Rings

For every bowl of pinto beans you serve, you'll need an extra roll of toilet paper, so why not use what you've got? Save some dried beans and hold on to your empty toilet paper rolls. In no time, you'll be able to whip up a beany table decoration that even your fiber-phobic guests will love.

What you'll need:

Cardboard tubes from toilet paper rolls or paper towels

Dried pinto beans and small white beans

Clear water-based satin finish craft paint (optional)

Shelf paper with peel-away sticky backing

Hot glue gun

1. Stuff your cardboard tube with newspaper for support and use a serrated knife to cut $1^1/2$-inch-wide rings.
2. For each napkin ring, cut rectangles $2^1/2$ by 6 inches from shelf paper. These will cover the inside of the ring. It is important for the inside of the napkin ring to be smooth, since the napkins slip in and out.
3. Cut across each napkin ring and flatten into a rectangle. Peel off shelf paper backing to reveal the sticky side. Cover the inside of the napkin ring, folding excess paper to the front and trimming as needed.
4. For each napkin ring, cut a strip of shelf paper about $1^1/2$ inches wide and long enough to close the napkin ring back into a circle.
5. Using a hot glue gun, attach beans, one or two at a time, to cover the outside of the napkin ring. Trade off using pinto beans and white beans if you feel like gettin' fancy.
6. To protect the napkin rings and help keep 'em around a while, paint the bean side with a clear water-based craft paint.

Chapter 4

WASH DAY DINNERS

Wash day gives new meaning to multitasking. Back in the day when washers and dryers as we know them didn't exist, the women of the house set aside a day, usually a Monday, to wash, wring, and hang to dry all the accumulated dirty laundry from the previous week. It was a lengthy job, usually taking most of the day to complete. While the clothes were washing, the ladies would pull together an easy-to-prepare evening meal, usually one that could be left to simmer on the stove or bake in the oven.

When my mother was a little girl, she used to help her mother do the laundry in an old wringer washer located right smack in the middle of the kitchen. While her mother cubed up a pile of new potatoes, Mom would fill the washer with water, add a little detergent, and turn on the machine to start the agitator. Once the agitator was going, she'd add the laundry. When the clothes were fully cleaned, each piece would be lifted from the water and run through the wringer (similar to running sheets of pasta through the roller of a pasta machine) and then dropped into a clean rinse tub. Then, back into the wringer the clean clothes would go, one last time, until finally the whole lot ended up hanging on the line to dry in the backyard.

In the meantime, the dried beans would be picked through for soup, corn would be shucked for pudding, and apples would be sliced and submerged in lemon water for pie. The iced tea would be made, the table set, and bread would be baking in the oven. Sometimes a little Bill Monroe played in the background while the women worked. It made for a long day, with as much of the meal being made ahead as possible. They'd chat, cook a little, and gossip. And, Lord knows, country people love their gossip, so I suspect all their hard work was paid for in juicy stories.

Once the laundry was finished and hung out to dry on the line, the last-minute cooking would be done—ham would be fried and coffee brewed for red-eye gravy. Finally the men would come home covered in coal dust from another long day in the mines, their lunch pails empty and the aroma of salty pork frying up in a cast iron skillet quickening their step. Nothing was better than putting on a fresh pair of overalls and digging into a hot meal after a hard day's work.

The Savvy Host Gets It Done Ahead

About 15 minutes before your guests arrive, light up a couple of smell-good candles. Make sure to have a big one lit up in the bathroom in case Grandpa Eddie shows up.

Make as much a day ahead as you can. For instance, make up your bread the day before and store it in an airtight container. Mix up your casseroles a day ahead and put 'em in the fridge, then bake 'em the day of.

Set up your table with fancy digs well before your guests arrive. Provide specific place settings, especially if you're worried Miss Viola won't get on too well with Miss Wilma.

Now, spritz up your "do," put on your swankiest, freshly washed outfit, and relax before your guests arrive.

Make your meal in a big ole pot. A pot of beans, a pot of soup, or a pot of greens makes serving up your meal super easy. Just cook 'em and leave 'em on the stove until your guests arrive. Save any leftover pot likker for makin' shooters after dinner.

NANNY'S NEW POTATOES IN BUTTER-CREAM GRAVY

My Great-Granny Charity was an immense woman who loved to cook mounds of hearty country food. She lived in a small coal mining town just outside of Welch, West Virginia, and during the early 1900s, often kept miners as boarders in her home. Since nearly everybody was on a budget back then, the meals Charity cooked were nourishing while easy on the pocket. Her food could keep a man going for many long hours over a mile deep.

    1 (5-pound) bag red or white new potatoes, scrubbed (keep the peels on!)
    6 to 8 tablespoons butter (don't use margarine!)
    2 to 3 tablespoons flour
    1 (12-ounce) can evaporated milk
    1 cup whole milk
    Salt and pepper, as much as you like

Cook potatoes in a deep pot of water, then set aside in a big bowl. Save 1$^1/_2$ cups of the potato cooking water for later.

Make gravy by melting the butter in a pot, stirring in some flour, a little at a time, and cooking for 3 to 4 minutes on low heat. Slowly add in your evaporated milk and your whole milk and some of the potato water you've saved aside. Stir the mixture quickly to keep lumps from forming, and continue cooking until the mixture starts to thicken up. Mash up a couple of the cooked potatoes and add them into the gravy. Add salt and pepper the way you like it. Cut the rest of the potatoes into quarters and add them to gravy. Serve up your hot potatoes to a tableful of hungry eaters.

ANAWALT COAL CAMP SOUP

1 pound onions, sliced
1/2 pound smoked ham, cubed
1/2 cup butter
3 cloves garlic, minced
3 pounds potatoes, cut into cubes
1/2 cup tomato paste
1 1/2 gallons chicken stock

1/2 pound rice
Salt and pepper, as much as you like
Spices of your choice, such as
    marjoram and a bay leaf (optional)
Parmesan cheese, for garnish
1/4 cup chopped fresh parsley,
    for garnish

Sauté your onions and ham in butter in a big pot. Throw in your garlic. Next, dump in the rest of your ingredients and simmer 'til your potatoes and rice are fully cooked. Add salt and pepper the way you like it, and any spices. (We like dried marjoram and a bay leaf.) Top your soup with Parmesan cheese and chopped parsley.

This soup makes enough for the whole family, plus plenty more for leftovers or freezin'.

GREASY RIDGE COCONUT CUSTARD PIE

5 eggs
2 cups sugar
1 (12-ounce) can evaporated milk
2 tablespoons butter, melted

1 tablespoon vanilla extract
1 1/2 cups sweetened flaked coconut
1 (9-inch) unbaked pie crust

Turn on your oven to 425 degrees.

Beat your eggs. Then add in your sugar, evaporated milk, butter, vanilla, and coconut and mix together real good. Pour into your pie shell. Wrap foil around the edges of your pie to keep it from browning too much and stick the pie in the oven for 15 minutes. Then take down your heat to 350 degrees and bake for another 25 to 30 minutes, or until set.

SECOND-DAY MEAL—NANNY'S NEW POTATO CHICKEN CASSEROLE

Second-day meals were always a staple in our home. Whatever was left from dinner the night before would be reshaped, refried, rebaked, and generally reconditioned into a completely different meal. The motto was nothing is wasted, and eating the same exact thing again is just plain boring. This recipe uses any leftovers you might have of Nanny's New Potatoes in Butter-Cream Gravy (page 32), adds a few ingredients, and comes out with something just as delicious.

Leftover new potatoes
Leftover chicken, cut
   into small chunks
2 tablespoons pimiento
Leftover butter-cream gravy

2 tablespoons butter, melted
Crushed buttery crackers mixed with
   crushed potato chips, enough to
   cover the top of your casserole

Turn on your oven to 350 degrees.

Slice up your potatoes and mix with chicken chunks and pimiento. Add the leftover butter-cream gravy to hold everything together. Use more milk if you think the gravy's too thick. Wipe down a casserole dish with a little shortening, and pour in your potato mixture. Cover with the butter and crushed cracker and chip combo. Heat just until bubbly, 15 to 20 minutes.

WILMA MAY'S GRANNY SMITHS IN A BLANKET

Cinnamon candies are thought of as another spice where I come from. You'll find a big bag of them sitting right next to the ground nutmeg and ginger. Add a handful to your cooked apples and you'll experience a sweet, cinnamony flavor unlike anything else.

1 1/2 cups sugar, plus more as needed
1 1/2 cups water
1/4 teaspoon ground cinnamon,
   plus more as needed
1/4 teaspoon ground nutmeg
20 hot cinnamon candies

1 tablespoon butter, plus more for topping
2 (9-inch) unbaked prepared pie crusts
6 Granny Smith apples,
   peeled and cored
Vanilla ice cream, for serving

Turn on your oven to 425 degrees.

Make up a syrup with the sugar, water, cinnamon, nutmeg, and cinnamon candies. Bring to a roaring boil over medium-high heat, then immediately take it off the heat and drop in your butter. Stir it all real good to make sure you dissolve the candies.

Cut each pie crust into 3 wedges (thirds) and wrap the apples, leaving the hole on top exposed. It doesn't have to be perfect, just cover the apple. Put your crust-covered apples in a baking dish.

Sprinkle on a little sugar and cinnamon and put a dab of butter into the hole of each apple. Pour the hot syrup over the apples. Bake for about 50 minutes, basting with the hot syrup every 10 to 15 minutes. If the liquid appears to be getting too thick, add a little water to thin. Serve warm with vanilla ice cream.

VIOLA'S FIERY THREE-BEAN HOT POT

A great way to get your dried beans to cook a little faster is to submerge them in cold water and then bring the water to a boil for 1 minute. Drain your beans and cook as usual. This extra step will cut down your overall cookin' time.

1 cup dried kidney beans	1 cup spicy salsa
1 cup dried pinto beans	1 tablespoon brown sugar
1 cup dried black beans	1 teaspoon ground cumin
1 large onion, chopped	1/2 teaspoon salt
1 large green bell pepper, chopped	Shredded Cheddar cheese
1 large can chicken broth (6 cups), plus more as needed	

Cook up your dried beans and then drain 'em, saving the liquid. Sauté the onion and green pepper until soft. Then add all of your ingredients to a large pot and bring up to a boil. Reduce your heat and simmer for about 10 minutes or so. Add more chicken broth or bean water to make it as thin as you want. Serve topped with shredded Cheddar cheese.

Clothespin Recipe Holders

How many times have you spilled sauce or splattered your recipe cards when cooking? Trying to cook with a recipe card sitting next to your minced onions and ground beef can be a real mess. Wouldn't it be much easier (and neater) to have your recipe hanging at eye level?

What you'll need:
6 ceramic magnetic discs, $1/2$ inch in diameter
3 wooden spring clothespins
Hot glue gun

1. Determine which side of the magnets attract the other.
2. Hot glue one magnet onto the flat side of a clothespin. Hot glue the second magnet to the inside of a cabinet door (preferably near your stove or working area) at cooks' eye level.
3. Select a door that can remain open while you cook. Stick the magnet and clothespin onto the second magnet and pin up loose recipes when cooking.
4. Repeat for the two additional clothespins.

Part Two

HOLY GATHERIN'S

Chapter 5

WHY THE ICE CREAM SOCIAL
SHOULD BE MADE ILLEGAL

The ice cream social is a simple recipe for childhood bliss, but like all good things, there is a fine line between ecstasy and evil. Any kid who has been to one of these socials knows what it can do; how its unmatched power can spawn an army of mini-sized wild, untamed gluttons within a matter of hours.

It goes like this. Take twenty chubby, gray-haired church ladies who are master cooks in their own right, organize a big picnic outside on a hot summer afternoon, complete with an array of sugar-laden sodas, homemade lemonade, brownies, cookies, pies, cakes, fudge, and, of course, ice cream. Then, add mounds of homemade ice cream, hand-churned by the chubby ladies themselves, all laid out on crisp paper tablecloths, decorated with plastic flower arrangements and matching paper napkins. Imagine all the important ice cream accessories at your disposal—nuts, cans of whipping cream, mini chocolate chips, crushed chocolate cookies, candy-coated chocolates, gummies, caramel sauce, and chocolate and strawberry sauces. Then, invite every kid in the neighborhood, ages three to thirteen, to come out and eat at will until they are one butterscotch sundae away from hospitalization.

As a young child, I often dreamed of being accidentally locked up in a 7-Eleven. My dream was this. Mom would take me to get some extra milk and then I'd hide out. She'd forget me, the store would close, and it would all be mine. I'd drink Slurpees straight from the electric churn, nosh on day-old cream horns, make cheese dogs from the rotisserie, and drink purple sodas until I got the shakes. But the real fantasy came from the candy aisle. I'd go shelf by shelf, starting with chocolates, then move on to the chews, the lollipops, and finally end with the chewing gum. It was a beautiful dream, but still a dream, until the day I attended my first ice cream social.

When I arrived, it was as if the pearly gates had opened up to reveal my future. All the church ladies were lined up, rows and rows of them, each with a giant metal ice cream scoop in her hand, just waiting for your sugary request. Want a double scoop? No problem. Want to mix chocolate sauce and Captain Crunch cereal into your peach ice cream?

No problem. Want to eat two or three bowls of ice cream at the same time while trying to suck down a chocolate shake? No problem. Want soda with that? How about some crumbled brownies on top? M and M's? Colored sprinkles? Want to experience your first case of lactose intolerance? Just say "more."

So, off I went, my parents unaware that I was about to embark on my first taste of a deadly sin, gluttony, and that I was going to do it on church property, no less. I stepped in line behind my best friend, Ellie, who, in between licking clean her Styrofoam ice cream bowl and plastic spoon, whispered, "You gotta try some of the Snicker's bar ice cream. It's full of candy bar pieces, really big ones. Mrs. Shaver will give you a big scoop. Don't tell anybody." She went back to scraping her bowl clean.

"How many bowls have you had?" I asked.

"Lost count after I hit Miss Treeda's," Ellie replied.

"What's she got?"

"She's got this caramel ice cream stuff that she puts Oreos and whipped cream on."

I cocked my head and savored the thought of that combination for a moment. "Oh yeah. That's gonna be good. Really, really good."

And so I hit up Miss Treeda and Mrs. Shaver for a double scoop each. Eventually, I moved onto cones (I had already gotten too used to the bowl) and then went on to cooking up my own concoctions by stirring together half melted chocolate ice cream with various candy toppings. It wasn't long before other kids caught on and began mixing up their own stuff, too. But I took it one step further, topping mine off with shots of strawberry soda, pieces of pecan pie, and anything else I could score.

Finally, I had to hit the bathroom. I walked past the giant mirror and noticed out of the corner of my eye that I had a perfectly shaped chocolate ring around my mouth. I stopped and peered closer. I was pale. I smelled weird. There were strange stains on my shirt, and when I finally smiled, I saw that one of my molars was blacked out by a chunk of Oreo. This is what I have become, I thought. This is my destiny. I'm an ice cream addict.

The rest of the kids continued to line up as the afternoon waned, forty to fifty deep at times, all jones'n for just one more bowl, one last frozen fix. Some would just be standing there, bug-eyed, hands shaking, sweat beading on their upper lips. Some would be dancing in line, like they were about to wet their pants, just itching to get up to that last bucket of homemade vanilla. They'd yell, fuss, and push each other, creating mini sword battles with their plastic spoons. I believe it was the choir director's son, Bobby Jr., who heaved onto the newly planted boxwoods in front of the auditorium, but it was hard to tell. I didn't recognize him anymore. It was chaos, a sort of pandemonium that only mass quantities of sugar could create. For the first time in my life, at the young age of twelve, I was witnessing the very fabric of our society unravel before my eyes. Soon, all that was left were piles of Styrofoam bowls dripping with the remnants of ice cream creations that only children could dream up.

As the day drew to a somber close, parents carried away their children kicking and screaming in fits of withdrawal. Watching the scene before me, even I considered just one last bowl for the road. Just one more scoop. Just enough to hold me 'til dinner.

⁊

ELLIE'S STRAWBERRY ICE

2 cups water

$^3/_4$ cup corn syrup

$1^1/_4$ cups sugar

1 quart ripe strawberries

1 tablespoon lemon juice

Make a syrup by mixing up your water, corn syrup, and sugar together in a pot and heating over medium heat until syrupy. Then mash up your strawberries and strain 'em into a bowl through a cheesecloth. You should have about $1^1/_2$ cups of juice. Add your strawberry juice and lemon juice to the cooled syrup and freeze in a metal loaf pan covered tightly with tin foil.

MISS TREEDA'S FLORIDA MILK SHERBERT

Mix together 2 cups boiled milk with 1 cup sugar. Cool. Mix up the juice of 3 lemons with the juice of 3 oranges. Add the juice mixture to the milk mixture, and stir in 3 diced-up bananas. Pour into a metal loaf pan and cover tightly with foil. Put it in the freezer until frozen and ready to eat.

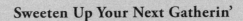

Sweeten Up Your Next Gatherin'

At your next gatherin', make it a requirement for everyone to lick their bowl clean. Take your party a step further by having your guests bring along their favorite bowls—the bigger the bowl, the longer the lickin'.

Let your kids have as much sugar as they want and then watch 'em go. Laugh out loud as they lip-synch to your old 8-tracks and choreograph their own set of dance moves. This can provide hours of family fun. But beware of impending stomachaches and sugar withdrawals. Sweeten up the fun by providing the youngins with instruments such as spoons, washboards, and harmonicas so they can create their own old-timey string band. Be sure to have plenty of earplugs on hand for the adults.

Create a sundae bar. Load up on every fixin' you can imagine, including the standards: nuts, candies, chocolate sauces (use a crockpot to keep your sauce warm), and colored sprinkles. And don't forget to throw in a few special ice cream yummies, like a big bowl of Jell-O jigglers, a couple of cans of cherry pie filling, a box of Captain Crunch cereal (keep it in the box—cereal is best when eaten by hand out of the box), or a jar of vanilla frosting with a plastic knife stuck in it. Then, let your guests stuff it in until they're so full of refined sugar they start gettin' the shakes.

Invite the church ladies. Have them whip up one of their favorite ice cream desserts (it's common knowledge that church ladies make the best treats) and then have them oversee the spoonin'.

Make sure your social takes place in the dead heat of summer, especially if you're in the South. There's nothin' better than snackin' on an ice cream cone that melts faster than you can eat it. And always remember, safety first. Keep a first-aid kit handy for accidental spork cuts, sudden head freezes, and latent sugar withdrawals.

SISSY'S VANILLA CUSTARD ICE CREAM

1 cup sugar

Just under 2 tablespoons flour

$^1/_3$ teaspoon salt

2 eggs

1 pint milk

1 pint heavy cream

$1^1/_2$ teaspoons vanilla extract

Mix together the sugar, flour, and salt. Beat your eggs until light. Add $^1/_4$ cup of the milk to the eggs and then add this to the sugar mixture. Heat the cream and the rest of the milk just to boiling over medium heat and add this to your sugar mixture. Cook it all in a double boiler for about 20 minutes, stirring constantly so your custard stays nice and smooth. Strain, cool, add the vanilla, and freeze. To make a gallon, just double up on these amounts.

Variation:

To make strawberry custard cream, run 1 pint of fresh berries through a ricer and sweeten 'em with a cup of sugar. Add the berries to the custard along with the vanilla.

DARLIN' SAVANNAH'S CHOCOLATE-DIPPED RITZ BITZ

This is the kind of dessert only a child could dream up. Take something that is somewhat good for you and coat it in chocolate. Any cookie or cracker will do, but the peanut buttery saltiness of the Ritz Bitz cracker is the perfect dipper for a vat of melted chocolate.

1 (9-ounce) package milk chocolate (cooking chocolate)

Peanut butter Ritz Bitz crackers

Melt up 4 blocks of the chocolate in a double boiler. Stir until fully melted. Dip crackers in melted chocolate. Shake off any excess chocolate and place crackers on waxed paper to cool.

BAPSOUSED BUTTERSCOTCH BROWNIES

1 (6-ounce) package (1 cup)
   butterscotch morsels
$^1/_4$ cup butter
1 cup packed light brown sugar
2 eggs

$^1/_2$ teaspoon vanilla extract
1 cup flour, sifted
$^3/_4$ teaspoon salt
1 teaspoon baking powder
$^1/_2$ cup chopped pecans

Turn on your oven to 350 degrees. Grease up your baking dish.

Melt up your butterscotch morsels and butter in a double boiler (or white-trash it by settin' a bowl over a small pot of boiling water). Then, take it off the heat and stir in your brown sugar. Let cool for about 5 minutes or so.

Next, add in your eggs and vanilla. Then mix together your flour, salt, and baking powder and sift it into your egg mixture. Stir it up real good. Stir in the pecans at the end. Spread into your baking dish and bake for 20 to 25 minutes. Cool and cut into tasty, sweet squares.

Gettin' Bapsoused

One of the more important rites of passage as a young child growing up in the Baptist church was gettin' bapsoused, or baptized. While some churches do a sprinkling of water on the head or some sort of mock submersion, we got the complete dunking. When my day came, like everyone, I wore my favorite underwear and bra underneath the required full length, translucent white choir robe. I eased into the lukewarm water in front of the entire congregation, witnessing the water rise above my waist. As the preacher gave the blessing and laid my body gently back into the water, he tenderly covered my mouth and nose with a dry handkerchief to keep any water out. The choir was singing and the congregation was rejoicing when I slowly rose from the water, cleaned and purified. I walked out of the water, my white robe clinging rather provocatively to my half-underdeveloped body. As I exited the baptismal, I happened to notice a few blue-haired ladies in the front row looking a bit shaken. When I smiled at them they turned their heads in awkward embarrassment. It was then that I looked down. All was righteous that Sunday morning, and it would've been perfect, if I had only worn white underwear.

Obscenely Large Fake Ice Cream Centerpiece

Fool your friends and get plenty of laughs with this spectacular ice cream creation. While this massive sundae may look good enough to eat, it's really made from plastic, Styrofoam, paint, and pipe cleaners. A true treat for the eyes and not for the tummy, this centerpiece will undoubtedly be the talk of your next ice cream social. Note: This is a more advanced craft and not one for beginners.

What you'll need:

Serrated knife

1 large plastic bowl (to hold your "sundae")

3 small plastic soup bowls (one each for "hot fudge," "cherries," and "whipped cream")

5 or 6 (1-inch-thick) Styrofoam disks (for the bottom of your bowls)

25 (1-inch-diameter) Styrofoam balls (for "cherries")

5 (2 1/2-inch-diameter) Styrofoam balls (for small scoops of "ice cream")

10 (3-inch-diameter) Styrofoam balls (for large scoops of "ice cream")

1 box wooden toothpicks

3 brown pipe cleaners (for "cherry stems")

1 container vinyl-based spackling compound

Acrylic paints (choose colors you like for your ice cream, cherries, hot fudge, and whipped cream)

Clear gloss enamel

Hot glue gun

To make the ice cream sundae:

1. Using the serrated knife, cut the 2 1/2-inch and 3-inch balls in half.
2. Coat the outside of the balls with spackle and allow them to dry.
3. Place a few Styrofoam disks in the bottom of the large plastic bowl and stack your ice cream balls on top. Build your ice cream mound by using toothpicks to attach the Styrofoam "scoops" together. When your ice cream mound is complete and to your liking, cover it with the spackling compound to suggest fake fudge. If you have any cracks, let the spackle dry, and fill in with more compound.
4. Paint your ice creams balls with desired colors, saving the hot fudge for last. Finish your fudge by painting it with clear gloss enamel.

To make the bowl of cherries:

1. Coat the outside of the 1-inch Styrofoam balls with spackle and allow them to dry.
2. Put on a second coat of spackle, wet your fingers, and smooth the surface. Let dry completely.

3. Paint each ball red. Let the paint dry completely, then coat with clear gloss enamel. Let this dry completely.
4. Insert a pipe cleaner (or "cherry stem") into each cherry and stack your cherries in one of the small bowls. Hot glue them together so they stay in place. Hot glue a plastic spoon into the bowl.

To make the bowls of hot fudge and whipped cream:

1. Place two Styrofoam disks in the bottom of two small plastic bowls. Cover with spackle to create a bowl of hot fudge and a bowl of whipping cream.
2. While the spackle is still wet, insert a plastic spoon into each bowl.
3. Let dry and respackle any cracks that have formed.
4. Let dry again, and paint one with brown and the other with white paint.

SWEET ASHLYN'S STRAWBERRY SAUCE

Take a bunch of fresh strawberries and cut 'em into quarters. Put your strawberries and a little water in a saucepan and cook on low heat until your berries start to soften. Add in some sugar, as much as you like, but make sure you melt it good so your sauce isn't grainy. Now, flavor your sauce how you like it. Add in some chopped mint or a squeeze of lemon to jazz it up, or do like the Italians and drizzle a little balsamic vinegar into your sauce and then toss in a pinch of black pepper.

Serve your sauce over your favorite ice cream. I still think vanilla works best.

DIETER'S DELIGHT

We country folk aren't exactly known for living the light and healthy lifestyle. But it's important to note that this Dieter's Delight contains no fatback, no butter, no bacon grease, and no lard, so for us, it's diet food.

2 cups cottage cheese
1 (20-ounce) can crushed
    unsweetened pineapple,
    well drained
1 (3-ounce) box orange gelatin

Chopped walnuts, if desired
1 large 8-ounce container frozen
    whipped topping

Place the cottage cheese in a large bowl and add the pineapple. Mix well. Add the gelatin and nuts and stir. Fold in the whipped topping. Refrigerate overnight.

Chapter 6

WEDNESDAY NIGHT SUPPERS—
FRIED CHICKEN AND TORPEDOS

For Wednesday night church suppers, the resident church ladies took care of serving up dinner, cafeteria style. We'd all line up, they'd spoon it out, and off we'd go to stuff it in. Nothing fancy. Nothing extraordinary. Except for Mary Jo Moxley. Miss Moxley was a master cook who was a little too well endowed up top. Put it this way. You couldn't miss them. Imagine two giant torpedos ballooning out from underneath a stretched-tight pink polyester knit sweater. Now, imagine this spectacle displayed on a 5-foot 2-inch, 70-year-old woman with a larger-than-life demeanor.

Miss Moxley's appearance made for easy jokes: "What she got under there? A couple of bald guys?" or "Those boobs are so big they could be used as a flotation devices." Over the years, the jokes lessened a bit until the Wednesday night when we were promptly reminded of her natural attributes in a rather unexpected manner.

Our whole gang was lined up in usual fashion with outstretched trays. Miss Moxley and her crew had just spent all day whipping up a more-than-special dinner of buttermilk fried chicken, macaroni and cheese, angel biscuits, and ambrosia salad. We were just dying to get at all that homemade food, and as everyone was gettin' their plates filled, my daddy (a.k.a. Mr. Bailey) asked one of the church ladies if he could have a chicken breast since he didn't care too much for the dark meat. He was swiftly informed that there were no chicken breasts left and that he had his choice between legs and thighs. Disappointed, he took a couple of thighs, as did I, and we began to walk over to our assigned table. But just as we were about to sit down in a roomful of a hundred fellow churchgoers, including pastors, deacons, and the minister of music, Miss Moxley came running in wearing her signature pink polyester sweater and greased-stained apron with boobs a-bouncin'. As she ran toward us, her gazongas nearly rebounded off the bottom of her double chin. Jaws hit the floor and children hid their giggles as Miss Moxley held up a piece of fried chicken in each hand and exclaimed in a thunderous voice sure enough to wake the dead buried out back, "Mr. Bailey! Mr. Bailey! Don't sit down yet! I gotch yer two big breasts right here!"

Cooking It Up for Your Crowd

Speaking of buffets, more often than not, we'd all bring something to the table, whether it was a big pot of green beans or a skilletful of fresh cornbread. Granny was capable of doing it all, but sometimes even she needed a break. When you're just plain overloaded, make your gathering a potluck, and have your guests do some of the work. Just make sure they take their serving dish home at the end of the night or you'll be doing a heck of a lot of washing.

Casseroles come in handy when you're cooking for a tableful of hearty eaters since the whole meal (meat, starch, and vegetable) is neatly piled into one big serving dish. Granny used to heat up some leftover rolls and we'd serve ourselves buffet style. It's an easy-to-prepare, inexpensive way to feed the whole congregation.

When we get cookin' for a crowd, we always make a little extra, since in our family, there's always somebody comin' back for seconds. Throw in a few neighbors who love to pop by conveniently at dinnertime, and an extra place setting or two is always in order.

Whenever Miss Moxley fried up a batch of her Buttermilk Fried Chicken with Torpedo Gravy (page 50), she'd let her finished chicken rest on racks set on top of baking sheets instead of draining them on paper towels. When it came time to serve, she'd pop her chicken pieces, rack and all, back in the oven for a few minutes, just long enough for them to warm through. Her chicken was always nice and crispy on all sides instead of mushy on one side, since it never spent time draining on a damp towel.

Don't forget to do some good. The kindest ladies I've ever met have been the women of the local church circle group. Don't be afraid to start your own. Circle groups are a great way to enjoy some tasty fellowship while helping those around you who may be less fortunate, ill, or just need someone to talk to. Have your group meet monthly at a select location, and be sure to serve up a platter of Church Ladies' Circle Salad (page 53) with Ritz crackers.

POOCHIE'S BISCUIT BEAN BAKE

1 pound ground beef

1/4 cup chopped onion

1 envelope Sloppy Joe seasoning mix
(set aside 1 tablespoon of mix)

1 (31-ounce) can or
2 (15-ounce) cans pork and beans

3 tablespoons brown sugar

1/2 cup ketchup

1 (12-ounce) can refrigerated biscuits

1 cup cubed Cheddar cheese

Turn on your oven to 350 degrees. Grease up a casserole pan.

Sauté your ground beef in a little oil until fully cooked. Drain off the fat unless you like it in there. Add the onions and sauté a little longer. Add your Sloppy Joe mix (except for the 1 tablespoon you're setting aside), your pork and beans, brown sugar, and ketchup. Simmer it for a couple of minutes until bubbly. Pour into your casserole pan.

Unroll the pack of biscuits. Open each biscuit and place a cube of Cheddar cheese inside. Do this for each biscuit. Place biscuits on top of the bean mixture. Sprinkle the rest of your Sloppy Joe seasoning mix over the biscuits and bake for about 30 minutes. Serve hot.

TATER TOT CASSEROLE

2 pounds ground beef

1 onion, diced

1 (15-ounce) can mixed vegetables,
with half of the liquid drained off

1 (11-ounce) can cream of
mushroom soup

1 (11-ounce) can cream of celery soup

1 (8-ounce) package Velveeta cheese,
cut into cubes

1 (1-pound) bag frozen tater tots

Turn on your oven to 350 degrees.

Brown up your beef and onion. Drain off the fat. Spread in a casserole dish. Mix together your canned vegetables, canned soups, and cheese. Spread this over the beef mixture and top the whole concoction with your tots.

Bake for 1 hour, or until your tots are browned and your casserole gets all bubbly.

MISS MOXLEY'S BUTTERMILK FRIED CHICKEN WITH TORPEDO GRAVY

1 frying chicken, cut into pieces

1 cup buttermilk

Flour

Salt and pepper, as much as you like

$^1/_2$ cup butter

$^1/_2$ cup shortening

Paprika

$^1/_4$ cup water

$1^1/_2$ cups evaporated milk,
   more as needed

$1^1/_2$ cups whole milk

Reba May's Creamy Mashed Potatoes
   (page 133), for serving

Angel Biscuits (page 52), for serving

Make sure your pieces of chicken are all the same size and are on the small side. If the breasts are too large (as they can often be) cut 'em into halves. Two to three hours before you plan to fry, rinse the chicken and put it in a large sealable plastic bag with the buttermilk. Store in the refrigerator until ready to cook.

Take a brown paper bag (a grocery bag is good) and put enough flour to easily coat the chicken in it. Add salt and pepper the way you like it. Remove your chicken from the buttermilk and put it into the paper bag. Shake your chicken up good and get ready to fry it. Save your flour mixture for making gravy later on.

Melt equal parts butter and shortening in a cast iron skillet. Have your heat at medium to medium-high, but be careful not to burn the butter. When the pan is hot, drop your chicken in the pan and brown on each side. Sprinkle paprika on each side along with salt and pepper the way you like it. Cook for about 20 minutes. Reduce the heat to medium-low, add the water, put a lid on the pan, and steam the chicken for 15 to 20 minutes. Take off the lid and continue to cook the chicken on each side to crisp it up again. Place the chicken on a rack to drain.

Scrape up the little crispy pieces from the bottom of the pan. Add 2 to 3 heaping tablespoons of the flour mixture from the paper bag. Stir, scrape, and cook for about 3 minutes. Add equal parts of evaporated milk and whole milk to the mixture and stir real good. You should have about 3 cups of liquid. Bring up to a low simmer. Continue stirring until your gravy thickens (the secret to a first-rate gravy is good drippings and fast stirrin'). If you find your gravy is gettin' too thick, add a little more evaporated milk. Add salt and pepper the way you like it. Serve up your gravy with a mound of mashed potatoes and hot biscuits.

SUNDAY CHURCH SUPPER CASSEROLE

Along with tasty midweek fellowship and some soul-satisfying Bible study, make sure you've got a mess of Church Supper Casserole to go around. Open up your canned soup and vegetables to whip up this easy, inexpensive one-dish dinner. And be sure to make this meal with an extra dash of pure love because you never know when you're going to be blessed with a miracle.

1 pound ground beef, browned and drained	1 teaspoon salt
1/2 cup chopped onion	3 cups mashed potatoes (homemade or instant)
2 (14-ounce) cans mixed vegetables, drained	Paprika
1 can cream of celery soup	Butter
1 teaspoon Italian seasoning	1 cup Parmesan cheese

Turn on your oven to 375 degrees.

Add your ground beef and onion to a large casserole dish. Throw in your mixed vegetables, celery soup, Italian seasoning, and salt. Mix it up good. Spread the mashed potatoes on top. Sprinkle with paprika and dot with bits of butter. Sprinkle Parmesan cheese over the whole shebang. Bake, uncovered, for 30 to 40 minutes, or until bubbling around the edges.

ANGEL BISCUITS

These biscuits are truly heavenly. Light and airy, they will melt in your mouth. What makes these biscuits so fluffy is the yeast, which gives the biscuit a less flaky and more breadlike texture. And here's a little hint my granny once told me: Avoid twisting off your can or biscuit cutter when you're cutting up biscuits as it can keep your biscuit from getting a good rise.

1 package active dry yeast	2 tablespoons sugar
2 tablespoons very warm water	1 teaspoon salt
5 cups flour	1 cup shortening
1 teaspoon baking soda	2 cups buttermilk
3 teaspoons baking powder	1 egg white, whisked

Turn on your oven to 400 degrees. Grease up a baking sheet.

Dissolve your yeast in a bowl with the warm water. Let it stand for about 5 minutes, or until foamy. If it doesn't foam too much, use it anyway. Your biscuits will still be delicious. Sift the flour, baking soda, baking powder, sugar, and salt together in a big bowl. Cut in your shortening using 2 knives. Make sure you have small grains of shortening. Now, add your buttermilk and yeast mixture. Turn onto a lightly floured board and knead gently for a minute or so. Don't worry if your dough is a little sticky. And be sure to go easy on the flour.

Roll out your dough to about an inch thick and cut your biscuits with the open end of a clean tin can or with a biscuit cutter. Brush the tops of each biscuit with a little egg white. Put your biscuits on a baking sheet and bake for 12 minutes, or until golden brown on top. Heavenly!

CHURCH LADIES' CIRCLE SALAD

Churches have always had special clubs, or "circles," as they are known, specifically designed for the women of the church. These ladies' groups meet monthly to plan the many ways they can help those in need, like visiting the sick at the local hospital or making up a batch of homemade cookies for an elderly shut-in. During these meetings a little coffee and tea might be served alongside a light dish of gelatin salad. This recipe was very popular in our church circle group. Made with lots of cream cheese and lemon gelatin, it's richer than your average Jell-O and excellent served with Ritz crackers on the side. To make your Circle Salad extra fancy, make it in a gelatin mold and unmold it atop a platter of lettuce leaves.

2 (3-ounce) boxes lemon gelatin

2 cups boiling water

1 (8-ounce) package cream cheese, softened

1 (8-ounce) can crushed pineapple, drained

3 to 4 tablespoons diced pimientos

$1/2$ cup lightly crushed pecans

1 cup heavy whipping cream

Dissolve your gelatin in boiling water. Let it stand a few minutes and then add cream cheese so it will partially melt in the gelatin. It's okay if you have a few cream cheese chunks in there. That's what makes it good.

Add in your drained pineapple, pimiento, and pecans. Mix well and refrigerate just until it starts to set. Then stir it again. Whip up your whipping cream and fold it into the gelatin mixture. Throw the whole thing into a baking dish and stick it back in the fridge so it sets up.

Homemade Paper Flower Arrangements with Sparkle

I bet you remember making paper flowers in elementary school. Well, these are no different. Set these homemade flowers out as a fancy centerpiece at your next gathering. Just make sure to store your flowers covered so they don't get dusty and fade.

What you'll need:

1 package dried small white beans
1 clear container for your arrangement
1 block floral foam to fit inside arrangement container
1 package tissue paper in mixed colors
1 package long wooden skewers
1 roll green floral tape
1 small jar white glue
1 small jar silver or gold glitter
1 sheet leaf-green craft foam rubber
Black permanent marker

1. Put 1 inch of beans in the container and add floral foam. Add more beans to fill the container and completely hide the floral foam.

2. Select 5 sheets of tissue paper in the same or different colors. Stack the sheets and cut 2 sets of 6-inch squares. Combine both sets to make a stack of 10 squares.

3. Trim 2 opposite edges of the stack by cutting 6 scallops along each side.

4. Starting with the straight side, fan-fold the stack into a rectangle with scalloped ends, about $1/4$ inch wide and 6 inches long.

5. Cut a 6-inch piece of wire and wrap it tightly around the center of the rectangle. Leave enough wire to attach a flower stem.

6. Form one half of the flower by carefully pulling each sheet to the center. Repeat this process for the other half.

7. Wire the flower to a skewer and wrap the wire and skewer with green floral tape.

8. Run beads of glue along the outer edges of the flower and sprinkle with glitter. Shake off any excess glitter and let dry.

9. Arrange flowers by poking skewers into the floral foam. Skewers may be cut to desired lengths.

10. Cut leaf shapes in a variety of sizes from the foam rubber. Using the marker, draw veins on the leaves. The leaves may be used to fill in blank spaces in the arrangement. Put a wire through the base of the leaf and attach it to the stem.

Chapter 7

AFTER-CHURCH ENTERTAINING—
WEST VIRGINIA RAT TALES

I must admit that my favorite part of going to church was leaving church to head home to partake of a gluttonous, post-Sunday worship service meal. I'd be sitting in one of the back pews while the blue-hairs fanned themselves with rolled-up Sunday bulletins and the preacher sermonized all about hellfire and damnation (always in the nicest of terms). The congregation would wail in appreciation as the choir burst into joyful song. While everyone in the house was feeling empowered by the presence of the Holy Ghost, I would suddenly have the need to dive into a big plate of Mama's creamed chipped beef on toast. The thought of mopping up that leftover gravy with a day-old cornstick sustained my soul until the clock struck twelve and out of the church's double doors we all spilled to fill our bellies with good food and wholesome family fellowship.

My daddy must have felt the same way, because as a young man, every Sunday right after church he'd head straight over to the Cypher's house in Possum Hollow. The Cypher's house was one of the few left at the time that was built from hand-hewn timbers. It rested right smack in the middle of the hollow, just steps from the cool, flowing Buckeye Springs. A small, makeshift gristmill in the old barn stood not far from the house near rows of freshly planted corn. Next to it was a small chicken coop where a couple of stocky hens provided fresh eggs. They even had a guard dog named Buckshot, who spent most of his days sleeping in the sun, and who frankly wouldn't know a burglar if one walked up and smacked him in the head. This was self-contained living. Everything the Cyphers needed to live existed on their property, so they rarely had to leave except when it came time for Sunday church. This was their way of life and they were more than happy to relinquish the world outside.

One Sunday, Daddy walked the two miles to the little house, conveniently showing up just as all the food was being laid out on the dining room table. Ramona Cypher, the matron of the house, did all the cooking, and on this particular Sunday the food was as good as it had ever been—creamed chipped beef on toast, boiled potatoes in pork broth, refrigerator slaw, and Daddy's favorite cornsticks, or as he called 'em, corndodger sticks.

Ramona's corndodger sticks were not your average cornbread treat. Miss Ramona took her cornbread making to another level ever since her husband, Roddy, started grinding up his own yellow meal straight from the cornfield. They'd shuck and dry the corn, and then Roddy would grind it up in his electric grain mill in the old barn behind the house. During the late summers, corn would be so plentiful that the meal would literally be piled up to the ceiling of that old, rickety barn. And it wouldn't be uncommon, on a hot afternoon, to see old Buckshot out there, tongue hanging out, lying in a big pile of it, trying to cool off.

But this post-church Sunday meal was set to be an unusual one. Daddy took himself a seat at the end of the table next to Sonny, the Cypher's only son, who hadn't uttered a single word since he was kicked in the head by a feral horse when he was ten years old. Sonny may not have had much to say, but he sure did love to eat. Instead of expressing himself in words and sentences, Sonny instead chose a combination of "mmm's," "aah's," and "yumm's" to show his gratitude. Pair these utterances with a drawn-out burp, and in his own way, Sonny gave vocal thanks for his meal.

Out the food came, steaming in metal pots and on cracked serving platters. As usual, Sonny began helping himself and promptly got his hand whacked for not waiting until the blessing was said. The four of them held hands across the table as Roddy offered up his usual Sunday afternoon prayer. "Before we eat this food, dear Lord, we bow our heads to pray; and for your blessings and your care our humble thanks we say." "Ayemen!" was announced and the food passing began. First the creamed chipped beef went around, then Ramona came on with the pot of boiled potatoes and took her big fork and plopped a couple onto everyone's plate. Next up was the refrigerator slaw with its unusual tang since it was made with a vinaigrette-style dressing completely devoid of mayonnaise. Last was everyone's favorite treat, the corndodger sticks, made with the cornmeal Roddy ground himself out in the barn. Served up with a stick of butter, they were just a bit salty and just a bit crunchy on the outside while hot and crumbly on the inside. True perfection.

Everyone ate their mounds of chipped beef, potatoes, and slaw, and just as Daddy was about to reach in and get another cornstick, Sonny began making more than his usual "oohs" and "aahs" at the table, and then his voice suddenly got louder and, for a moment, it sounded as if he was trying to formulate an actual word. "Rahh...Rahh," he kept repeating. "What is it, Sonny?" Ramona asked. Daddy went ahead and picked up another cornstick and proceeded to eat it. Sonny pointed at the cornstick still in Daddy's hand and, this time even louder than before, exclaimed, "Rahh...Rahh!" He jumped up and down in his seat, screaming "Rahhh! Rahhh!" and still pointing directly at Daddy's cornstick. "You want a cornstick, Sonny?" my daddy asked. Sonny emphatically shook his head no, folded up his arms, and looked away. "Okay, then. Suit yourself." And with that, Daddy took a big bite.

Just as he was about to swallow, Daddy felt something stick in his front teeth. He reached up and pulled out a single, short black hair. Sonny jumped up and started pacing back and forth with excitement, half laughing and half crying, pointing at what was left of my daddy's corndodger stick. "Rahhh... Rahhh...Rahhhhht!"

Daddy examined the little black hair still in his hand a little closer. Sonny's "Rahhh, Rahhh," began to mutate into "Rat! Rat!" as we all finally started to catch on. It was rat hair—which meant only one thing. Rats love corn and Roddy makes his own meal from corn in the barn. A rat must've made an unexpected trip through the electric mill, then into the cornmeal batter, finally establishing its eternal resting place in a towel-covered basket on the dinner table. It was an implausible explanation that only living deep in the holler could bring. And with that, the only table guest to enjoy any more cornsticks for the rest of the evening was old Buckshot.

⇛

BLASPHEMIN' ON A SHINGLE (CREAMED CHIPPED BEEF)

3/4 stick butter (no substitutes)

1 (3-ounce) jar chipped beef (feeds 2 to 3 people)

2 to 3 heaping tablespoons flour

1 large (12-ounce) can evaporated milk

1 1/2 cups whole milk

1 cup water

Salt (optional)

Pepper

Biscuits or toasted bread, for serving

Melt up your butter in a cast iron skillet. Tear the chipped beef into pieces about the size of postage stamps. Brown your chipped beef in the butter until it's crispy. Sprinkle the flour over the beef and stir for about 3 to 4 minutes, until it clumps together.

Slowly add the evaporated and whole milks. Then add the water, stirring really fast to get rid of the lumps. Cook until the mixture starts to get thick. Don't add salt until you take a taste as the beef is already salty. You can add plenty of pepper. Serve over biscuits, toasted bread, or whatever you have on hand.

NANNY ANNIE'S BOILED POTATOES IN PORK BROTH

During the Second World War, my daddy lived with his paternal grandmother and her live-in nanny, "Annie," in a small farmhouse just outside of Bluefield, West Virginia. One of his most cherished memories was diggin' into some of Annie's homespun cookin', which often consisted of a mess of collard greens, cornbread, and her famous pork broth boiled potatoes. They'd stuff themselves silly and then gather in a small adjacent bedroom to listen to the cathedral radio until it was time to go to bed. Those may have been simple times, but for him, never did so little money provide so much good eating and fellowship. My daddy is always quick to remind me, especially in these days of excess, that you don't need much to have a lot. This recipe is also great with rutabagas. Add rutabagas like you do the potatoes and cook a bit longer until tender.

2 meaty pork ribs	3 or 4 good-sized potatoes,
1 quart water	cut into quarters
	Pinch of salt and pepper

Put your ribs and water in a saucepan and cook over medium heat until the ribs are about half done. This should take about 60 minutes. Then add your potatoes to the broth and cook until done but still a bit firm to the fork. Add salt and pepper the way you like it.

OLLIE V.'S GINGERBREAD

This gingerbread recipe is super-old, and goes back to our German roots. Serve it up by itself or whip up a little cream with some vanilla and drop a big spoonful right on top.

1 cup molasses	1 teaspoon baking soda
1/2 cup butter, softened	1 teaspoon ground cinnamon
1/2 cup very hot water	1 teaspoon ground ginger
1 egg, beaten	1/2 teaspoon ground allspice
1 cup flour	

Turn on your oven to 350 degrees. Grease up an 8-inch square baking pan.

Stir up your molasses, butter, and hot water and add your egg. In another bowl, mix up your dry ingredients. Add your molasses mixture to your dry ingredients and mix everything up real good with a wooden spoon. Scrape the batter into the pan and bake for about 20 minutes, or until a knife inserted comes out nice and clean. Serve warm with a dollop of fresh cream.

After-Church Eatin'

Make most of your Sunday meal on Saturday. Since you can't very well skip church to stay home and cook on Sunday morning, make as much as you can the day before and have it ready for reheating.

Whatever you eat, make sure it's fattening. As a good, Southern churchgoer, you probably can't drink, smoke, or fornicate, so you might as well load up on caffeine, sugar, and fats. Barbecue, butter, and bacon are all condoned by the church, so dig in.

Before you head out to church, whip up a batch of Nanny Annie's Boiled Potatoes in Pork Broth (facing page) in your crockpot. Set it on low and let her roll. Add your potatoes after you get home so they don't go all mushy.

Don't work so hard. Host a Sunday supper out. Take the family out to the local cafeteria or the all-you-can-eat-buffet steakhouse. Get your butt in line with everyone else and eat yourself silly. Don't forget to stuff any extra rolls and butter packets in your purse for later.

Always remember that the biggest meal of the week (we call it "supper") can only take place after you've spent at least a full hour sittin' in church, so put on your Sunday best and get comfortable 'cuz you're gonna hear the sermon first.

RAMONA'S REFRIGERATOR SLAW

This slaw boasts everything a tasty cole slaw should have except for one classic ingredient: mayonnaise. Made with a cider vinaigrette, this tangy slaw is the perfect blend of tart and sweet. Make this a day ahead as it needs at least a full 24 hours in the fridge to come together proper.

1 large head cabbage
1 green bell pepper
1 red bell pepper
$^1/_2$ small sweet onion
   (add more if you like it)

DRESSING
1 cup apple cider vinegar
1 cup sugar
$^2/_3$ cup vegetable oil
1 teaspoon dry mustard
1 teaspoon celery seed
1 teaspoon salt

Shred the head of cabbage and chop it up. Slice a few thin green and red pepper rings to put on top of your slaw before serving it up, then dice the rest of the peppers and the onion. Mix those in with the cabbage.

To make your dressing, mix up your vinegar, sugar, and oil in a pan and bring it up to a boil. Turn off your heat and stir in your mustard, celery seed, and salt. Pour dressing over the cabbage mixture while it's still a bit warm and mix it up good. Top with your sliced peppers and stick it in the fridge overnight.

BUTTER-FRIED GRIT CAKES

Warm up a mess of leftover cooked grits (see page 134) in the microwave. Add a little water to 'em if you need to thin 'em out. Heat up your cast iron pan and add a scoop of butter. Pour a little grit mixture into the bubbling butter and cook until golden brown. Then give it a flip and do the other side. You'll probably need to add more butter, but that's okay because everything is better with butter. Don't worry if your grit cakes fall apart. They're still tasty!

Corndodger Warmers

What you'll need:
4 clay saucers, the kind that go under 6-inch ceramic flower pots
4 large cloth napkins

1. Put your clay saucers in a 350-degree oven while everyone is setting down for grace, and heat 'em for about 10 minutes.
2. Then take 'em out of the oven and put a cloth napkin in each. Make sure everyone gets a warmer before the corndodgers are passed around.
3. Use your corndodger warmers to keep any hot bread warm during your meal.

DADDY'S CORNDODGER STICKS

Make up a batch of K.G.'s Country Grit Bread (page 24) and pour into your cast iron cornstick pan. Bake 'em up as you would regular cornbread; just remember that the sticks take a little less time. Make sure to pick your cornmeal clean before using!

Chapter 8

CHRISTMAS DINNER
AT GRANNY BOOHLER'S AND
GRANDPA WOODY'S HOUSE,
OR WHY WE DON'T NEED MANNERS

My Granny Boohler and Grandpa Woody lived in a two-bedroom mini rancher up a hill somewhere in Mercer County, West Virginia. The house couldn't have been more than 1,200 square feet total, including the extra-wide screened porch, but somehow every Christmas we would pack in eleven aunts, uncles, and cousins who not only ate three meals a day there, but slept there—on couches, floors, blow-up mattresses, you name it. For three days, we would knock into one another, vie for bathroom privacy (which was nonexistent), and generally lie around like a pile of sweaty hogs waiting for our next meal. There wasn't much to do up there as you can probably imagine, so our activities ranged from eating, to eating, to more eating.

Ever so often, my daddy and uncle would break out their guitar and banjo for a little predinner bluegrass jam, and for about a half hour, we'd put the TV on mute and sit around the plastic Christmas tree trying to put together words and chords to classics like Lester and Earl's "Salty Dog Blues." Sometimes we'd all take turns trying to hit that one yodeling high note in Bill Monroe's "Mule Skinner Blues" ("Good morning, Captain. Good morning, son!"), which none of us could do except for Daddy. Once in a while, Granny would pop her head around the kitchen door, wearing her signature red Christmas apron and request something gospel, so we'd sing a few off-key chords of "Angel Band" by the Stanley Brothers, which always made her smile and tear up just a bit. But before we could get through the first verse of "Rank Strangers," Granny would call us into the dining room to experience her version of the gospel—Christmas dinner. With enough food to feed an entire congregation, Granny would hustle and bustle back and forth from the kitchen to the dining room (a three-foot walk) laying out a mishmash of foodstuffs—whole glazed hams, cooked green apples (from an apple tree in the back-yard), collard greens cooked in fatback, mounds of white turkey gravy, creamed corn, sweet potatoes, gelatin salads, and homemade apple butter. And this was only the first round. Food literally spilled out onto the back porch where more of it rested on picnic tables and fold-out chairs, wrapped loosely in tin foil and packed into beaten-up plastic Tupperware containers.

When we finally sat down to eat, the table was usually still being set. (Patience was not considered a virtue when it came time for dinner.) All eleven of us would reach for goodies off the relish tray (olives, pickled vegetables, carrot sticks, and a big spoonful of onion soup mix dip) but no one dared touch the big stuff until Grandpa gave the blessing. Grandpa Woody would then commence to bless the food with the most melodious prayer of thanks one could imagine—a prayer that compelled the angels in heaven to weep with gratitude. His words echoed off the fourteen-pound turkey, the three applesauce cakes, and the oversized bowl of sugary cole slaw.

And then we would eat. Arms and elbows collided as each family member reached for the same dish on the table. Hands got slapped for reaching too far. One of my cousins would have already finished his meal, pushed away his chair, and would be sitting in the living room watching TV before I even got my first bite of curly kale. Ever so often, the English language would surface in some mutated form with, "Gimme dat" or "You done wid dem beans?". The sound of dulled, stainless-steel knives stabbing an already dwindling slab of butter was our only music now, and faint grunting from both ends of the table made up for conversation.

After dinner, we'd all spill into the living room and begin tearing at our Christmas presents. And just like with dinner, it was every man for himself. But you had to work fast. If you didn't get to your present in time to open it yourself, it very well could be opened by someone else since about half of our presents were wrapped without gift cards. I'd grab the biggest box and tear it open only to find a naked-from-the-waist-down G.I. Joe doll staring back at me in all his trouser-lacking glory. I'd then stand up and shout, "Okay, who gets this?" One of my cousins would reach over and grab the doll, annoyed that I had gotten to it first and it was missing a decent pair of fatigues. But everything would fall back into place when that same cousin enthusiastically ripped open the wrapping on Barbie's Dream House.

There were leftover gifts—pairs of mismatched gloves, boxes of outdated chocolates, a set of six ice scrapers for the car, old Christmas ornaments. These same exact gifts somehow made it under the tree, each and every year. They'd be opened, tossed aside, and subsequently forgotten. After we had all gone to bed, Granny would take these rejected gifts and seal them up in a big box in the attic. The following Christmas she'd take out the box, rewrap all the same gifts, and place them back under the tree. And once again, we would gullibly tear them open with excitement, letting out a sigh of frustration when the star mint candies were lifted out of the can in one solid block. It was as if these poor lost Christmas presents existed in a state of gift purgatory, forced to relive being re-wrapped, torn open, and ultimately rejected year after year.

Our day of holiday gluttony would usually end with a big bowl of freshly popped popcorn (Granny loves her popcorn) and a marathon of made-for-television Christmas movies. We'd pile up on the couch, surrounded by a sea of shredded wrapping paper and pass around that big bowl of popcorn properly doused with melted butter. It was almost always snowing outside, and the windows would frost from the bottom up, making the whole scene very Norman Rockwell. Yet, it was those moments, with all of us huddled together, that we were an unbreakable union of kin in the purest sense. And although some of our family has since passed on, the rest of us are left with immaculate memories of singing bluegrass out of tune, opening gifts without names, and waiting patiently to hear the melody of Grandpa's blessing.

☙

COLONNADE ESTATE WALDORF SALAD

Juice of 1/2 lemon

2 apples, diced

1 cup chopped celery

1/2 cup broken walnut meats

Mayonnaise

Iceburg lettuce, for serving

Pimiento, for garnish

Squeeze your lemon juice over the cut-up apples and mix with celery and nuts. Add enough mayonnaise to hold the ingredients together. (Granny Boohler always adds a ton.) Stick it in the fridge. Arrange your fancy salad on iceburg lettuce leaves and garnish with strips of pimiento.

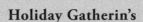

Holiday Gatherin's

Granny always made too much food. She had two packed-to-the-gills refrigerators filled with turkey, ham, cheese balls, gelatin salads—you name it. We'd find new ways to rearrange things just to pack in one more dish of sausage dressing. When that didn't work, we started laying out food on the back porch. If it gets cold at Christmas where you live, feel free to maximize your back porch—just make sure it's enclosed, so the critters don't get to your dinner before you do.

Granny took regifting to a whole new level with most of her recirculated gifts coming from the post-Christmas bargain bin at the local department store. Digging through a pile of heavily discounted Christmas ornaments can be very profitable, but the key is to buy in bulk. Don't buy just one nativity set, buy ten—this way everybody in your family can be on equal standing as they receive the same exact gift. Take it a step further by rewrapping these gifts and giving them out to the family again the next year so they can relive the holiday experience again.

Christmas was always meant for sharing at our house. If I didn't get a chocolate sampler and my uncle did, I'd help myself to his. We all had the "what's mine is mine and what's yours is mine" philosophy. Even when I poked out the bottoms of all the chocolates to avoid the jelly one, nobody seemed to care. And by New Year's, everyone would have had at least one of my "retouched" chocolates. I think my family considered my sampling a big favor, since by displaying the insides of each one, I made their chocolate selections so much easier.

Manners were always optional at Granny's house, and rarely enforced. We double-dipped, bogarted the butter knife, and picked off each other's plates when nobody was looking. But we all knew better than to do any of this in front of Grandpa, since so much as sniffing one of those hot biscuits before he blessed it resulted in a good slap on the hand.

Making a proper bowl of popcorn is an art form. Nearly every holiday meal ended with popcorn. To make yours the West Virginia way, get out a large cast iron pot and heat about 4 tablespoons of corn oil on high. Pour in enough popcorn to cover the bottom in one even layer and put the lid on. Shake the pan constantly so your kernels don't burn. Once they've all popped, melt up a generous amount of real butter (no margarine here!) and pour it all over the top. Add as much salt as your blood pressure can stand. Then, curl up under a big blanket with the whole family and dig in while watching "A Christmas Story" three times in a row.

ZURLEKA'S HOLIDAY CHEESE BALL

It just ain't a holiday without a cheese ball. I've seen 'em rolled in nuts, coated in store-bought bacon bits, studded with shrimp, and laced with pimientos. Whatever makes your ball special is up to you. Surround your fancy ball with a fan of buttery crackers, and it'll be gone before the end of your first Christmas carol. If you want, you can make two smaller cheese balls out of this recipe instead of one bigger one.

2 (8-ounce) packages cream
  cheese, softened
2 cups chopped walnuts
$1/4$ cup minced green bell pepper
2 tablespoons minced onion

1 (8-ounce) can crushed pineapple,
  well drained
$1/4$ teaspoon salt
$1/4$ teaspoon black pepper
$1/4$ pound bacon, cooked and crumbled
Minced fresh parsley, for garnish

Mix up your cream cheese with 1 cup of your walnuts, your green pepper, onion, crushed pineapple, salt, and pepper. Add your crumbled bacon and stir to combine everything well. Roll this mixture into a ball. Now roll your cheese ball in the rest of the walnuts. Sprinkle with a little minced parsley. Wrap in plastic and chill in the refrigerator until ready to serve.

Snacky Time Punkin' Seeds

Wash your seeds real good. Strain 'em through a colander and then dry them on paper towels. Grease up a baking sheet really well and spread the seeds on it, then toast your seeds at 350 degrees for 20 minutes or until they are crunchy and light brown. Add a little salt, black pepper, and cayenne pepper (if you can stand the heat). Store in a glass jar on your countertop for easy snackin'!

OVERKILL-ON-THE-TURKEY TURKEY

Here's how we do it. Cook your turkey early, so you'll have room in your oven later for side dishes. To start, take out the giblet bag and wash out the cavity of your turkey real good. Pat your turkey dry and then sprinkle salt and pepper and rub butter all over in the inside and outside of the bird. (Push butter pieces up under the skin so your turkey will self-baste.) Stuff with dressing or do as we do and cook your dressing separately. Fill your turkey instead with quartered onions and pieces of celery.

Cook your turkey in a roasting pan breast side up in a preheated 400 degree oven for about half an hour. Then lower your oven heat to 325 degrees. Pour a couple of cans of chicken broth into the bottom of your roasting pan and put a piece of aluminum foil around your turkey in a loose "tent" fashion to keep the wings from burning.

Your cooking time should reflect the size of your bird. Estimate a 20-pound turkey at around 5 to 6 hours. Make sure to baste your turkey with the pan drippings at least once during the last 2 hours of cooking. In the last 45 minutes of cooking, remove the foil tent and turn your turkey upside down (breast side down) so the dark meat juices run into your breast, making it nice and juicy. Leave off the foil tent at this point. Your turkey is done when a poultry thermometer inserted into the thickest part of the breast reads 165 degrees, or the legs begin to feel all loosey-goosey when you tweak the end of a drumstick.

Let your turkey set a good 30 minutes before carving. Save your pan juices for gravy.

OLEANA'S SAUSAGE DRESSING

We mountain folk don't like calling dressing "stuffing" since we rarely actually stuff it in the turkey. We call it "dressing." The dressing is supposed to be nice and crispy on the outside, not mushy and wet. Get your dressing even crispier by baking it in muffin tins with everyone getting an individual serving.

1 tablespoon shortening
1 pound spicy sausage
1 1/2 cups chopped celery
1 1/2 cups chopped onion
3 (15-ounce) cans chicken broth, plus more as needed for consistency
1 stick butter
1 (1-pound) bag cornbread stuffing mix, plus more as needed for consistency
1 (1-pound) bag cubed herb stuffing mix, plus more as needed for consistency

Melt up your shortening and fry the sausage on low to medium heat. Keep breaking up the sausage as it fries 'til it is about the size of small peas and gets nice and crispy. Set aside, saving two tablespoons of sausage grease.

Turn on your oven to 350 degrees.

In a separate pan, cook the celery and onion in the sausage grease 'til tender. Add the 3 cans of chicken broth. Add the butter and heat until it melts. In a large bowl, combine the sausage with the broth mixture and both stuffing mixes. Stir up lightly with a fork. Your dressing should be moist, not soupy. Like all great recipes, this one is not an exact science. If your dressing gets too soupy, add more dressing mix. If it's too dry, add more broth. Put the dressing in a large casserole dish and bake for 20 to 25 minutes or until brown and crusty on the outside. Time it so the dressing goes in the oven just as you take the turkey out and prepare to let it set on the stove to rest before carving. Then everything will be hot and ready all at once.

SHINY POLE BEANS

We call these beans pole beans because they were originally planted at the base of old wooden poles so the vines would grow upward for easy pickin'. These beans work best for slow cooking because of their thick outer skin. A nice variation to this recipe is to add cut-up potato wedges during the last 20 minutes of cooking time or until tender but not mushy.

2 to 3 pounds pole beans
Large slug of salt fatback, or 1 to 2 meaty pork ribs
4 ounces water

Snap your beans and remove their strings. Then break 'em into 2-inch segments. Drop your beans into a big ole cooking pot filled with water and let it get to a slow simmer. In the meantime, place your seasoning meat in a coffee cup with 4 ounces of water and microwave it on high for about 30 seconds. Turn the meat over and repeat for another 30 seconds. Pour your salt meat and water into your beans and cook over medium-low heat, covered, for about 2 hours. Stir your beans every now and then, but be careful not to break them apart. Drain 'em and season 'em the way you like 'em with a little salt and pepper.

Snow Ice Cream

Needless to say, it snows a lot up in the hills of West Virginia. If you have snow in your area, when your car, your lawn, or even your neighbor's dog gets covered with the white stuff, help yourself to it and make this tasty dessert. This is a great recipe for vanilla ice cream using actual snow. (Just make sure your snow ain't yellow.)

1 egg
1/2 cup brown sugar
1 teaspoon vanilla extract
1/2 cup heavy whipping cream

2 quarts clean snow
Chocolate chips, fruits (strawberries are
   good), or whatever else strikes your fancy

Mix your egg, sugar, vanilla, and cream in a bowl and pour it over a large bowl of snow. Add chocolate chips, fruits, or other additions of your choice before freezing. Stir it quick before it melts and put it in the freezer for later or eat it right out of the bowl.

GRANNY BOOHLER'S WEST VIRGINIA APPLESAUCE CAKE

There wasn't a Christmas that went by in our house without an applesauce cake. Granny always stored this delicious, moist cake in a tightly sealed plastic container filled with sliced apples from the backyard tree, so it never dried out. This cake tastes best when eaten Christmas morning with a cup of weak, Southern-style coffee and a mound of unopened presents with your name on 'em.

3 cups applesauce
2 heaping teaspoons baking soda
1 cup shortening (or $^1/_2$ cup butter and $^1/_2$ cup shortening)
$2^1/_2$ cups sugar
1 teaspoon ground cloves
2 teaspoons ground cinnamon
1 teaspoon ground nutmeg
2 cups raisins
1 cup chopped walnuts
$3^1/_2$ cups flour

Turn on your oven to 325 degrees. Grease up and flour a standard-sized bundt pan.

Heat the applesauce until it's piping hot. Add the baking soda while the applesauce is heating and stir it in. Cream up your shortening and add the sugar and spices to it. Add the applesauce to the shortening mixture and stir it around. Pour this mixture into a big bowl. Throw in your raisins and nuts and sift in the flour. Stir it all up together real good and then scrape the mixture into your bundt pan.

Bake for $1^1/_2$ hours, or until a knife stuck into the center of the cake comes out clean. Let the cake cool in the pan for at least 10 minutes before gently releasing it onto a cooling rack. Serve it at room temperature, and store in a tightly sealed container with plenty of sliced apples to keep it moist. You can store this cake in a cool place such as your basement for up to 3 weeks.

GRANNY B'S PUMPKIN PIE

There just ain't nothing better than a homemade pumpkin pie, and good ole Granny Boohler sure knows how to make 'em. She thinks the small sugar pumpkins make the best pies. Save your seeds for later as they make a great snack (see the recipe for pumpkin seeds on page 66). You can store cooked, mashed pumpkin in freezer bags and have it on hand for when you want to make pie. When you make this pie, try cooking two pumpkins at the same time and save half of the mash in the freezer for next time. You'll have the added bonus of even more pumpkin seeds to snack on now!

2 pumpkins (sugar pumpkins work best) or 3 cups cooked pumpkin
3 to 4 eggs
1^1/$_2$ cups sugar, plus a little more for the whipped cream
1^1/$_2$ cups evaporated milk
^{3}/$_4$ stick butter, melted
1^1/$_2$ teaspoons ground cinnamon
^{3}/$_4$ teaspoon ground cloves
2 unbaked prepared pie crusts
Heavy whipping cream and a little sugar

Turn on your oven to 375 degrees.

Cut the tops off of your pumpkins and scoop out all the stringy material and seeds. Save those seeds and throw the stringy stuff out. Put the tops back on your pumpkins and set the pumpkins in a baking pan filled with 3 inches of water. Bake until soft (1 to 1^1/$_2$ hours or until fork tender). Pour off the excess liquid, let 'em cool, and then peel your pumpkins and mash 'em well. You should have about 4 cups of pumpkin meat.

Turn up your oven temperature to 450 degrees.

Combine all of the ingredients in a bowl and mix 'em up good. A blender works best since fresh pumpkin can be fibrous. Pour into the pie shells and bake for 10 minutes. Then reduce the oven temperature to 350 degrees and bake for 30 to 40 minutes. Whip up a little fresh cream with just a pinch of sugar and top your pie with dollops of it.

Christmas Paint Can Wine Cooler

Paint buckets aren't just for paint anymore. After you clean and decorate your paint bucket you can use it as a cooking utensil holder, set it in the bathroom to hold extra toilet tissue, use it to hold paper towels, or fill it with ice and stick it on the dinner table with a bottle of wine stuck inside.

What you'll need:

One 1-gallon paint can in decent condition

Sandpaper

Paint suitable for metal surfaces, in desired base
  color (light colors work best)

1 (1-inch) paintbrush

Sheet of rub-on transfer designs or stencils (usually sold at arts and crafts stores)

1 tube of cement (to glue marbles to metal can)

1 bag of marbles (also usually available at arts
  and crafts stores)

1. Wash the paint can inside and out and sand down any rough spots.

2. Paint the can with a coat of color and let it dry.

3. Decorate your can using the transfer design, stencils, or your own drawings if you're artistic-like.

4. Glue the marbles around the top rim of the can and let them dry.

Part Three

POTLUCK
HEAVEN

Chapter 9

FAMILY REUNIONS—
WARRING MATRIARCHS, SHACKIN' UP,
AND COUSIN LOVE

In our family, there are three events that you just don't miss—your birth, your death, and the annual family reunion. Missing a wedding, a graduation, or a good birthing is somewhat forgivable. Just send a card picturing some puppies wrapped up in a blanket along with a wad of cash and all's well. But missing an annual family reunion is as blasphemous as blurting out the "F" word during the offertory prayer at Sunday church.

My granny puts tremendous effort into coordinating these annual family gatherings, which have taken place at just about every location you can imagine—from the dining hall in the Elk Creek Methodist Church to the overcrowded back room at the all-you-can-eat steakhouse in Princeton, West Virginia (complete with accordion-style "wood paneled" privacy walls). We've proudly displayed our family surnames within the brick halls of picnic shelter #2 at Hungry Mother's Park, in the cafeteria at the Salem Civic Center, and in Johnny's Restaurant, which is attached to the Mercer Motor Lodge where an outdoor sign still proudly declares it is "American Owned."

Granny Boohler is the family "kinkeeper"—our very own Mother Jones. She's the master of ceremonies at every event and her post is never challenged. For each yearly reunion, she happily handles all logistics, including location, food assignments, invitees, photographers (whoever's got a camera), attire, and, of course, all arm twisting, guilt laying, and threats of eternal damnation in order to make sure we are all there. She is the quintessential event planner—give her a shot at the Oscars, and there's no question in my mind that she could handle it—even at 95 years old.

Yet, even the best hosts have their quirks. One year, Granny decided that the family reunion would be held in her very own backyard, ironically a first, considering how much she loves having people over. It was one of those rare hot days in West Virginia, and what better way to celebrate summer than to hold an old-fashioned cookout. Assignments were given to those attending, and all the usual homemade suspects were in order: a big bowl of mayonnaisy potato salad topped with sliced hard-boiled eggs, green bean salad with plenty of sugar and vinegar, icy homemade lemonade, and vats of sweet tea.

But this time, Granny decided that instead of making this just a regular summer pot-luck, she would try her skills at the charcoal grill, whipping up a batch of burgers for the whole gang. Everyone was to bring a side dish that would pair well with her tasty burgers, but other than that, there was to be no additional meat (and we country folk don't like going a meal without some kind of meat). Add to that, West Virginia ladies aren't exactly renowned grill masters. They are the grand dames of the kitchen, and especially of the woodstove, but grilling just ain't their thing. Give my granny a couple of eggs, some flour, and some sugar, and she'll whip up the best cake you've ever eaten. Give her a searing hot grill, a pair of tongs, and a big bottle of lighter fluid, and you've got a ground beef disaster of epic proportions.

First, Granny got the grill going. After spraying out most of the can of lighter fluid, she threw a match to it. Flames reached up a couple of feet, and I swear they felt the heat forty minutes up the road in Beckley. Once the fire died down, and we had a chance to make certain we still had eyebrows, the simple burgers (nothing but salt and pepper on them) went onto the grill. The lid was shut, and that was it.

Granny made the rounds, pouring out fresh tea, picking up discarded paper plates, and posing for family photos. She cooed over baby pictures, pinched cheeks, and hugged grandsons. Meanwhile, the burgers cooked. She hand-washed empty casserole dishes, put on a pot of coffee, and retrieved jars of homemade jam from the basement. Meanwhile, the burgers cooked. She got out the croquet set, hit a few badmintons with the torn-up racket, and picked up lost golf balls. And all the while, the burgers cooked and cooked and cooked.

By this time, most of the side dishes had been finished, and folks were onto dessert and coffee. Smoke billowed, but no one really paid attention to it with all the hugging and kissing going on. Suddenly, Granny jumped up from her chair, let out a few "Lordys!", and ran over to the grill. She flipped open the top, and as smoke rose into the sky, we all walked over to witness Granny's very first (and last) attempt at making burgers on a charcoal grill. When the smoked cleared, eighteen barely discernable nuggets of charred meat were displayed in the midday sun. All but their intended roundness had melted away within the belly of that grill.

We patted Granny on the back, assuring her we were too stuffed to eat them anyway and not to worry since we thought burgers, on the whole, were overrated. She lowered her head for a moment, mildly perplexed. Then, as swiftly as the last poof of smoke dissipated into the afternoon sky, Granny perked up and announced to the crowd, "Burgers are served!" And with that, she carefully removed what was left of each burger, piling them high onto a clean serving platter. She set the platter down next to the sliced tomatoes, onions, and ketchup and stood back with her arms proudly crossed, resolutely undeterred by the fact that her platter of burgers looked like a mound of West Virginia coal. Her last words on the issue were softly muttered under her breath, "Well, the best part of the burger is the onion anyway."

℃

MEMAW'S DEVILED EGGS

Deviled eggs are a must at all covered dish gatherings, and this recipe is one of the best. For the perfect hard-boiled egg, gently place your eggs in cold water and put 'em on the stove. Bring eggs up to a boil. Just as they reach a boil, set your timer for 9 minutes. Drain the eggs and run cold water over them to stop the cooking. Works every time! Put out these tasty eggs, and I bet they'll disappear faster than a rabbit on the run.

1 dozen peeled hard-boiled eggs	1 teaspoon mustard
2 tablespoons sweet pickle relish	Pinch of cayenne pepper
2 tablespoons pickle juice (bread-and-butter pickle juice if you have it)	2 tablespoons mayonnaise
	6 stuffed green olives, cut in half
1/4 teaspoon salt	Paprika, for garnish

Slice up your boiled eggs the long way and pop out the yolks. Mash up your yolks, relish, pickle juice, salt, mustard, cayenne, and mayonnaise. Fill your eggs and top each with an olive slice. Lightly sprinkle with paprika and chill. These are best made a day ahead.

The Kinkeeper as Host

At our family reunions, as good Southern Baptists, we were never allowed to drink, but maybe you can. If you do, make sure to have a jug of homemade fruit wine on hand and a pony keg of Genny Cream Ale. If you're really from the mountains, bust out that Ball jar full of Grandpa's moonshine that you've been hiding—but go easy on it. Real moonshine has been known to make even the hardest of drinkers go a little blind.

Don't forget the burgers. Burgers and outdoor gatherings go together like warm biscuits and honey. Make your burgers by lightly shaping them (don't smush 'em down when you pat them into shape or they'll come out tough) and accenting them with just a little salt and pepper. And don't leave your burgers while they're sittin' on the grill. Your burgers should be lightly charred on the outside and warm and juicy on the inside. Slice up your onions in big thick pieces so your burgers stand high and proud on the bun.

Make it a covered dish affair. The covered dish is a whole different thing from the potluck. A potluck leaves the possibility of folks bringin' store-bought food. The covered dish is something you make at home, pour into your casserole dish, and stick a cover on. The covered dish almost always guarantees good food, especially if the grannies are cookin'. Plus, it's less work for you since everyone else gets to do all the cooking.

Make sure to have a little fun and games at your next gatherin'. We always had some kind of entertainment at our reunions like watching cousin Eugene win the pumpkin pie eating contest and then taking bets on how long it took him to puke. Whacking a few golf balls in the backyard has also been another popular pastime in our family, but make sure everyone aims away from the house. With that in mind, I recommend always choosing putters over woods.

No Southern family reunion is complete without at least one good reference to "The War Against Northern Aggression," or the Civil War, as others like to call it. If you're in the South, be sure to mention the Civil War at least once at your next family reunion. Remember those lost to "Yankee arrogance" by proudly recounting still-living family members who bear names like Surrenda Lee, who was an old friend's great, great aunt, born on the very day that General Lee surrendered.

GRANDPA CENTER'S BLACKBERRY SWEET ROLLS

This recipe is a three-parter, but is well worth the effort. Make up these "rolls" jelly roll style and bake in a sweetened blackberry syrup.

SYRUP

3 cups blackberries,
    washed and dried
1^1/$_2$ cups sugar
2 cups water

1 tablespoon butter, melted
^{1}/$_2$ teaspoon ground cinnamon
1^1/$_2$ tablespoons sugar
Vanilla ice cream or whipped cream,
    for serving

DOUGH

2 cups flour
2 teaspoons baking powder
^{1}/$_4$ cup sugar
1 teaspoon salt
^{1}/$_2$ cup butter, cold
1 egg
^{2}/$_3$ cup milk
^{1}/$_2$ teaspoon vanilla extract

Mash up 1 cup of the blackberries and combine with the sugar and water in a saucepan. Bring to a boil and simmer for 5 minutes. Turn off the heat and leave on the stove.

Meanwhile, make the dough by sifting the dry ingredients together into a bowl. Cut in your butter with a pastry blender or 2 knives. In a separate bowl, mix up your egg, milk, and vanilla. Add your wet ingredients to the dry ingredients and stir to combine. On a sheet of waxed or parchment paper, gently roll or pat out the dough to a 9 by 12-inch rectangle.

Turn on your oven to 450 degrees.

Brush the melted butter on the dough. Combine the cinnamon and sugar and sprinkle over dough. Spread the rest of the blackberries over the dough and roll up jelly roll style, using the long edge, and pinch to seal. With a piece of dental floss, cut 8 slices about 1^1/$_2$ inches thick.

Pour the hot syrup into a 9 by 9-inch baking dish or pan. Carefully lay the slices into the hot syrup and bake for 20 to 25 minutes. Serve warm with ice cream or whipped cream.

JUDY MAC'S DEE-LICIOUS
EASY PILED-ON PORK CHOPS

This is a-little-of-this and a-little-of-that kinda recipe with a tart/sweet sauce that just about makes itself.

8 ($1/2$- to 1-inch-thick) pork chops
Several lemons, sliced up
A couple white onions, sliced across $1/4$ inch thick
Brown sugar

Ketchup
Molasses
Salt and pepper, as much as you like
$1/3$ cup water

Turn on your oven to 350 degrees.

Put a little shortening in your cast iron skillet and brown the pork chops real good on both sides. Then put your chops in a deep baking dish. Now pile on the good stuff. Top each chop with a slice of lemon, a slice of onion, and a big tablespoon of brown sugar followed by a heaping tablespoon of ketchup. Drizzle some molasses over the entire dish and add a little salt and pepper. Then pour the water evenly over the whole dish. Bake in a hot oven until the sauce starts to thicken, about 1 to $1^1/2$ hours.

SWEETENED CONDENSED MILK
MACARONI SALAD

The way my Granny Boohler taught me to make macaroni salad was heavy on the mayo and light on the macaroni. This macaroni salad, although a little on the sweet side, has a better balance of mayo to macaroni—meaning, the macaroni isn't literally swimming in it.

6 cups dried macaroni

$1/2$ cup white vinegar

$1/8$ cup sugar

$1/4$ cup sweetened condensed milk

$1^1/2$ cups mayonnaise (or more to taste)

1 cup diced celery

4 carrots, grated

8 green onions, minced

1 green bell pepper, diced

2 cups shredded sharp Cheddar cheese (or more if you like it cheesy)

Cook your macaroni, and drain and cool it down real good. Put it in a big bowl. Mix together your vinegar, sugar, milk, and mayo in another bowl. Add a little salt and pepper if you think it needs it. Add your vegetables and cheese to the macaroni. Add in your dressing and mix it up well. Put it in the fridge to chill it up before serving. This is best made the day before.

Reunions: Cookie Gifts on a Stick

It's fun for everyone to take something home after a gathering. These reunion cookies serve as table decorations and as edible gifts for kin and friends.

What you'll need:
Popsicle sticks (available at craft stores)
Cellophane wrap or clear party bags
Pipe cleaners or wire closures
1 recipe Reunion Oatmeal Cookies dough, uncooked (see page 82)
Icing in a tube (the kind that sets up dry), any color

1. Drop a heaping tablespoon of dough, about the size of a large walnut shell, onto a baking sheet.
2. Poke a popsicle stick into the dough ball and press the dough around the stick to make a secure connection.
3. Ball up pieces of aluminum foil and place them under the end of the popsicle stick to keep the stick parallel with the baking sheet. Bake according to recipe directions.
4. Let the cookies set on the baking sheet and then move them to a wire rack to cool.
5. Once cooled, use icing to write and decorate each cookie with your family name or the year of your reunion. When your icing dries, cover the cookie with cellophane or put into party bags and fasten with a pipe cleaner.

REUNION OATMEAL COOKIES

2 sticks butter (1 cup)

1 cup white sugar

1 cup packed brown sugar

2 eggs

1 teaspoon vanilla extract

1 cup Rice Krispies cereal

2 cups uncooked oatmeal

2 cups flour

$1^{1}/_{2}$ teaspoons baking soda

$^{1}/_{4}$ teaspoon baking powder

1 teaspoon ground cinnamon

$^{1}/_{2}$ teaspoon salt

1 cup shredded sweetened coconut

1 cup white raisins

1 cup chopped pecans

Turn on your oven to 350 degrees.

Cream up your butter and sugars until nice and fluffy. Add the eggs and vanilla and mix 'em up real good. Stir in the Rice Krispies and oats. Sift the flour, baking soda, baking powder, cinnamon, and salt together into a bowl. Add this mixture to the sugar mixture and mix well. Stir in your coconut, raisins, and nuts. Put heaping tablespoons of the mixture on an ungreased baking sheet and bake for 12 to 14 minutes. You'll have about 5 dozen cookies.

LORETTA SILPAT'S SAUSAGE BALLS

Entertaining is a lot more fun when you don't have to work so darn hard. This recipe is a "classic" in our family. It has been brought to family reunions, potlucks, and church gatherings. These cute little balls have even been elegantly laid out on the table at Christmas with toothpicks stuck in 'em.

1 pound shredded cheddar cheese (real sharp cheese works best)

3 cups Bisquick mix

1 pound breakfast sausage (not links!)

Turn on your oven to 350 degrees.

Mix up your ingredients real well in a large bowl. Roll into small balls (about $^{1}/_{2}$ inch each) and bake for 15 minutes. Serve warm or at room temperature.

Once cooked, these can be frozen in plastic bags. Just thaw and reheat.

MISS CHARITY'S CRANBERRY CAKE
WITH ORANGE SAUCE

2^1/4 cups flour	1 cup buttermilk
^{1}/2 teaspoon salt	1 cup whole uncooked cranberries
1 teaspoon baking soda	1 cup chopped pecans
1 teaspoon baking powder	1 cup chopped dates
1 cup vegetable oil	Grated peel of three oranges
1 cup sugar	1 cup sugar
2 eggs	1 cup orange juice

Turn on your oven to 350 degrees.

Sift up your flour, salt, baking soda, and baking powder into a big bowl. In another bowl, beat the oil, sugar, eggs, and buttermilk. Add in your flour mixture to the egg mixture. Then throw in the cranberries, pecans, dates, and orange peel. Mix it up good.

Grease up a casserole dish and pour it all in. Bake your cake for 40 to 50 minutes, or until a toothpick stuck in the center of it comes out clean. Heat the sugar and orange juice in a small saucepan, just until the sugar is dissolved. Spoon over the warm cake. Let the cake sit overnight before cuttin' into it. It's cranberry-licious!

Chapter 10

WHEN IN DOUBT, GO WHOLE HOG!

The last time I had a real throwdown, hoedown-style pig pickin', I realized that the whole party is made up of three basic ingredients: a pig, a fire, and a bunch of guys who love to drink beer. The pig pickin' is the end-all, be-all party of parties. Think of it this way—it's hard to get any more country than designing a two-day party that focuses on one of our best loves: pork—all 100 pounds of it. Invite a mess of your closest friends, roll in a couple of kegs of cheapo beer, and party 'til dawn—literally. Most of your guests won't arrive until your pig is crispy on the outside and oozin' juice on the inside, but for true masters of the pig, the party is not in the eating, but in the twenty-four hours of cooking that takes place beforehand.

This is where the "guys who love to drink beer" part comes in. The first thing to do, other than setting the date, getting a pig, and assigning potluck dishes to your friends, is to call up a couple of pig "experts," or pit masters (or be the man yourself—just remember you will need help, so start recruiting your pals early). Your pit masters must live for cooking pig. When I asked one pit master why he would volunteer to slave over a hot fire all day and all night, he simply responded, "I live for this." And that he does. Guys like him literally count down the hours until the next time they can pull up their trucks and start roasting another pig.

Now, to get yourself a big ole pig, call up your local butcher or hit up one of your local farmers. Whole hogs can be ordered off the Internet, too. Just make sure your pig is split in half or butterflied before tossing it on the grill. You can do this yourself with a chainsaw or if you're faint of heart, get your butcher to do it ahead of time. And be sure to have a place to refrigerate your pig until your fire's ready since I doubt you can fit a 100-pound hog in your kitchen fridge. A rented refrigerated truck works well or simply have your pig delivered split and ready shortly before it's time to toss it on the fire.

To get the party started, break open a couple of Miller High Lifes, park your butt on the back of a flatbed truck, and plot your next move. The first order of business (and probably the longest part of the process) is firing up the burn barrel. We pile up cedar logs inside a beat-up, rusted metal barrel (fully equipped with a hole near the bottom for shoveling coal) and light the whole thing on fire. Then we let the fire burn down to glowing embers. When the wood is properly cooked down (this is often the up-all-night part since getting your burn barrel going takes about four hours), ruby-orange coals should be left at the bottom. Start with about twenty pounds of coals and shovel it along the bottom of your fire pit, adding a few more coals at each end where the shoulders and butt of the pig are. This will help your pig cook a bit more evenly since the shoulders and butt take longer.

Once the pig is fully split (longways, of course) and seasoned the way we like it, we put it split-side down onto the grill. To monitor the temperature of the grill, just place your hand directly on the side of the grill. If your hand burns, the grill is too hot, if your hand is barely warm, your grill is too cold. When you can leave your hand on the grill for just a second or two before it gets too hot to stand, the grill is just right (at about 220 degrees). Throughout this process, periodically baste the pig with your secret sauce (try a vinegar-based sauce like Wild Mountain Pig BBQ Sauce (page 88). Continue to shovel hot coals into the smoker as needed to maintain your temperature. You will do this for four to six hours before you flip it, depending on the size of your hog. Do your best to keep the grill closed; opening it often will greatly reduce your oven temperature. So, when the kiddies come over during the party to take a look at your fancy grilled pig, you must resist opening the grill. A consistent oven temperature is key to serving up a fall-off-the-bone hog at your intended dinner hour.

Now, what's truly vital to all of this hard work is to fully embrace the idea of sitting up all night and half the day with your buddies chatting, sucking suds, and sharing tall tales, because this endless shoveling and basting takes a long time. But you can't get too drunk. We once had a pit master who had a few too many 16-ouncers while he was in charge of basting and watching the fire and he passed out during the final hours of the pig roasting. He woke up the next morning to a really bad hangover, a pig that was blacker than Mingo County coal, and a bunch of very disappointed BBQ lovers.

When your pig is getting crispy on one side, it's time to give 'er a flip (this is a two-person job). Be sure to baste it again, and this time get really generous with the sauce. Cut deeply into the pig's ribs and into the tougher areas of the Boston butt, and pour your delicious sauce all over and into the cuts. Baste as often as you like, but remember what I said about opening the lid. Plan on roasting your pig another two hours or so or until the internal temperature reads 170 degrees.

A couple of hours later, your pig should be nice and tender on the inside and per-fectly skin-crisp on the outside. When your first round of guests begin to arrive, lay out their potluck dishes and anything else you had time to make. My favorites are Drunken Weenies (page 106), Miss Violet's Potato Rolls (page 90), and Burris Honeycutt's Cider Slaw (page 90). The craftier among your bunch can try their hand at making Chef Forky Pig (page 92) for a centerpiece. Throw on some bluegrass in the background and light a few citronella candles to keep the bugs away.

When your pig is good and done, get your pit masters to pull away the tender meat. We just dump the meat, sauce and all, into large foil bins. Every once in a while, squirt more sauce over the whole mess. Separate the Divine Miss White (the precious white meat) into another bin, and watch out for folks who start pinching off pieces with their hands. I don't think we've ever gotten a bin of white meat to the table before half of it was eaten. And remember, a properly executed pig pickin' can actually create a full-blown feeding frenzy, so you should expect plenty of nonstop pickin'. Therefore, always guard your grill.

Throwing a real pig pickin' is without a doubt the most generous way to show your family and friends how much you love their company. There's no other gathering that can match the sheer volume of food and fellowship that a pig pickin' offers. Pig pickin's are special times and go well beyond the average BBQ. An invite to a pig pickin' is rarely one that folks decline. These gatherin's come straight from the heart. It's a time to reunite with old friends, reminisce about old times, and enjoy one of the purest forms of cooking so unique to the South.

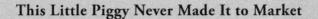

This Little Piggy Never Made It to Market

Pick your poison. Since your butt's gonna be sitting next to that pig all night, entertain yourself with a case of cheap beer and a big bottle of basting sauce. After every third beer, baste up the pig. Repeat 'til you finally pass out at daybreak.

Decide how you're gonna cook the pig—in a smoker, on a spit, or in a pit—it's up to you. However you do it, just make sure your pig isn't restin' directly on a pile of hot coals and that your temperature never exceeds about 225 degrees. You gotta cook it long and slow.

Don't even think of cooking up any more food. Make everyone else do it. You've already sacrificed enough. You sat up all night basting, you smell like burnt pig flesh, and you're drunk as a skunk and it's not even 8 a.m. Be sure to include the word "potluck" in your invitations. And don't forget the kids. Always have a few hot dogs and some ripples chips on hand for the kiddies.

Get yourself a big pig. Lucky for you, nowadays you don't have to kill one yourself. Just call up your local butcher or slaughterhouse, or go hunting on the Internet for a whole hog for roasting (a 100-pound pig will yield 40 to 50 pounds of meat).

When your pig is done, be the man and serve it up. Put on a pair of heavy-duty gloves and tear off the flesh from your fall-off-the-bone pig. Ladies may turn away in disgust and kids may burst into tears, but the rest of us will be standing in front of you with outstretched plates and drooling mouths.

WILD MOUNTAIN PIG BBQ SAUCE

This sauce makes a ton, but keep in mind you've got to baste a 100-plus-pound pig with it. Make sure to set some of this tasty sauce aside before you baste with it for topping sandwiches and platters of freshly smoked barbecue.

2 quarts cider vinegar
4 tablespoons Worcestershire sauce
4 tablespoons Tabasco sauce
4 tablespoons chile powder
8 tablespoons paprika
12 tablespoons black pepper
12 tablespoons salt

3 (32-ounce) ketchup bottles
3 teaspoons dry mustard
4 pounds brown sugar
2 cups water, or more as needed to achieve a
   sauce-like consistency
1 to 2 tablespoons dried ginger
12 Vidalia onions, chopped

Put all of your ingredients in a big pot and cook over medium-high heat for about 15 minutes, 'til all your flavors come together. Store in glass jars or empty ketchup bottles in the fridge for a day or two. Baste up your pig inside and out with this tasty sauce.

BBQ RIBS WITH ZYLPHA'S COKE-COLA SAUCE

2 racks spareribs, trimmed up of fat
Salt and pepper or your favorite
   grill seasoning
$1/8$ cup white vinegar
$1/4$ cup brown sugar

1 cup ketchup
2 tablespoons hot sauce
   (or more if you like it spicy)
5 ounces cola

Turn on your oven to 275 degrees.

Rub the ribs all over with salt and pepper and/or grill seasonings. Arrange ribs in a single layer in a roasting pan. Cover tightly with foil and roast 'em up for $2^1/2$ hours, or until the meat falls off the bone.

Heat up the vinegar, brown sugar, ketchup, hot sauce, and cola and simmer, uncovered, for about 10 to 15 minutes (the longer you simmer, the thicker it gets).

Take your ribs and slather them real good with the sauce. Throw 'em on a hot grill, basting with a little sauce. Brown 'em good on all sides. Serve up with any leftover sauce.

MOM'S BEST POTATO SALAD

Those of us who love to make (and eat) potato salad are convinced our salad is the best. Well, this recipe is no different. We think this potato salad is unsurpassed because of one special method—sprinkling the hot, cooked potatoes with apple cider vinegar, sweet pickle juice, and sugar. This extra step gives your potatoes a sweet and tangy flavor, setting your salad apart from the rest.

4 cups scrubbed and cubed red or
white potatoes (keep the peels on!)

1 teaspoon apple cider vinegar

1 tablespoon bread-and-butter
pickle juice

1 tablespoon sugar

$1/2$ cup chopped onion

$1/2$ cup chopped celery

$3/4$ cup mayonnaise

Salt and pepper, as much as you like

3 hard-boiled eggs

Fresh parsley, as much as
you like (optional)

Paprika, for garnish

Cook the potatoes in boiling, salted water. Drain your potatoes good, put 'em in a bowl, and sprinkle 'em with the vinegar, pickle juice, and sugar. Stir them around, being careful not to mash your potatoes. The potatoes should have a medium-tart taste with a hint of sweetness. Adjust to suit yourself, but remember the mayonnaise will make it sweeter.

Add the onions, celery, mayonnaise, and salt and pepper the way you like it. Chop 2 of your hard-boiled eggs and throw 'em in. Mix it all around again. Slice the third egg and use it to decorate the top, along with the parsley and paprika. Make this a day ahead for the best flavor, and no pickin' at it!

MISS VIOLET'S POTATO ROLLS

These delectable rolls may take a little extra time, but they're well worth it. Once you get the basic recipe down, you can shape the rolls into clover leaf or loaf shapes, or use them for cinnamon rolls (page 97). Serve toasted for breakfast with homemade jam or apple butter (page 7).

1 package active dry yeast
$1/2$ cup warm water
$1/2$ cup plus $1/2$ teaspoon sugar
1 or 2 white potatoes,
    peeled and cut in large pieces

$1/2$ cup shortening
1 teaspoon salt
1 egg
7 to 8 cups flour

Mix up your yeast, warm water, and the $1/2$ teaspoon sugar in a bowl and let stand at room temperature for 45 minutes. It'll get real foamy. Cook potatoes until tender in about 3 cups simmering water (enough to make $2 1/2$ cups leftover potato water). Mix your cooked potatoes and $2 1/2$ cups potato water in a blender. Add the $1/2$ cup sugar, shortening, and salt and blend it up real good. Add your egg and blend 5 seconds more.

Cool mixture to lukewarm. Then pour into a big ole bowl and add the yeast mixture. Slowly add 4 cups of the flour and beat with a mixer until smooth. Add 3 to 4 more cups of the flour and knead until the dough is fairly stiff but still a little sticky. Place in a greased-up bowl. Grease up the top of the dough and cover it with plastic. Then cover your bowl with a wet kitchen towel and place in the refrigerator for at least 8 hours. (The dough will keep for 5 or 6 days. Push dough down with the palm of your hand at least once a day.)

To bake the rolls, turn on your oven to 375 degrees. Grease up a baking sheet. Shape the desired number of rolls, place on the greased-up pan, and let rise in a warm place for $1 1/2$ to 2 hours, or until doubled in size. Bake for about 15 minutes, or until golden brown.

BURRIS HONEYCUTT'S CIDER SLAW

All good Southerners know you can't have a platter of barbecue without a heapin' pile of homemade slaw. This recipe is a classic blend of cider vinegar, sugar, and finely grated cabbage, and should be made to order since it doesn't set well in the fridge.

Finely grate about a half a head of cabbage.

Like lots of country-style recipes, the ingredients for the dressing have some flexibility according to your tastes, but we like to use a ratio of 4 tablespoons of sugar to 3 tablespoons of apple cider vinegar and then add about 3 to 4 tablespoons of mayo. Mix the sugar and vinegar until the sugar is completely dissolved. Add enough good mayonnaise (Hellman's is best) to make the mixture smooth and creamy.

About 30 minutes before dinner, combine enough of the dressing to coat the slaw and put it into the refrigerator for the flavors to blend. Season with salt and pepper the way you like it and serve up with a pile of pork barbecue and a side of baked beans.

CHELSEA'S SUMMER STRAWBERRY PIE

1 9-inch baked pie shell (page 154)
1^1/$_2$ to 2 quarts fresh strawberries
1 small (3-ounce) box
   strawberry gelatin

1 cup white sugar
3 tablespoons cornstarch
Pinch of salt
Heavy whipping cream

Get out your potato masher and pulverize ^{3}/$_4$ cup of strawberries. Add enough water to make 1^1/$_2$ cups liquid. Toss this mixture into a saucepan and stir in the gelatin, sugar, cornstarch, and salt. Cook over medium heat until thick and clear, stirring constantly, about 7 or 8 minutes.

While this mixture is cooling, cut up the rest of your strawberries. Spread one-third of the cooled mixture over the bottom of the baked pie shell. Put sliced strawberries in next and pour the rest of the cooked mixture over the strawberries. Cover and refrigerate for 2 to 3 hours, 'til set. Make up some fresh whipped cream and serve with a dollop on top of each piece.

Variation: Fairynette's Peachy Pie

Follow the recipe above, but replace the strawberry gelatin with peach gelatin and use 9 or 10 ripe peaches (peeled and sliced into 6 or 7 wedges each) instead of strawberries. The more peaches, the better; this pie is prettiest when the peaches mound higher than the crust.

Chef Forky Pig

Let Chef Forky Pig help host your next pig pickin'. Made from a plastic jug of apple cider vinegar, Chef Forky Pig holds plastic knives, forks, spoons, and napkins in his cute chef's apron. Just set Chef Forky Pig next to your plates and hot sauces and guests can serve themselves right from his little apron.

What you'll need:

1 cup beans or sand (enough to keep Chef Forky Pig stable)

1 gallon plastic White House cider vinegar jug

1 jar light pink paint (suitable for plastic)

1 jar red paint (suitable for plastic)

1 sheet pink craft foam rubber

Hot glue gun and sticks

Pencil

Black oil paint pen, thin point

$^1/_2$ yard black sailcloth or any denim-like material

1 apron with three pockets

1 yard $^3/_4$-inch black elastic

1 index card or stiff white paper

1 white paper towel

2 inches black fringe (optional)

Plastic eating utensils

1. Empty your unused vinegar into quart jars and rinse the jug real good to get rid of the odor. Study the plastic jug's shape to determine the head, snout, chest, and apron locations.

2. Put 1 inch of beans or sand in the jug to stabilize it, then screw on the cap.

3. Paint the face with the light pink paint and the chest area with the red paint. Do not paint the back of the head or the handle area.

4. Cut pig ears from the pink craft foam and hot glue them to the head.

5. Make the pig nose longer by gluing circles, cut from pink craft foam, to the snout area.

6. Sketch eyes and snout holes with a pencil, then outline with black oil paint pen.

7. Use black cloth to sew a tube to slip over the apron area. It covers its "hips" and "legs."

8. Make or buy an apron with three pockets to hold the eating utensils. Pin elastic to the apron and wrap around the pig's neck to support the weight of the eating utensils.

9. Cut a chef's hatband from an unlined index card to fit around the screw cap. A paper towel can be stuffed into the top of the hatband to form the puffy part of the chef's hat.

10. Black fringe can be added to look like hair.

11. Fill the apron pockets with plastic knives, forks, and spoons, and put your pig right next to a big pile of barbecue.

Chapter 11

COMFORTING COMFORTS— BALL JARS AND FUNERAL CAKE

As a child, I was lucky enough to have three grandmothers. My father's mother, Granny Boohler, my mother's mother, Granny Belcher, and my Granny and Grandpa Boohler's longtime neighbor and friend, Maw Maw.

Maw Maw lived in a small, brick, two-bedroom home, painstakingly built by her husband (known appropriately as Paw Paw). The home was about 100 feet from my grandparents' home (which Paw Paw had also built back in the fifties) and boasted a mini carport, a paved drive, and a big picture window fronted by expertly clipped rhododendrons (the West Virginia state flower). The property was neat as a pin—immaculately mowed and edged by Paw Paw, who took great pride in caring for his small plot of land.

Maw Maw and Paw Paw lived in Mercer County, West Virginia, where small towns such as Princeton and Bluefield still flourish along with nondescript in-between places bearing names like Possum Hollow, Greasy Ridge, and Punkin Center. Nearby was Junior's used car dealership along with the Air Strip Motel, owned by Maw Maw and Paw Paw's son, which, ironically, was nowhere near an actual airport. Up the street, you could get the best foot-long chili dog in town at the local Tasty Dawg. It was that kind of place.

Down the road a bit rested the old, beat-up yellow school bus that the Clemons family made into their home. Much in the same way a hermit crab makes his home out of an empty conch shell, the Clemons's made their home out of an abandoned school bus. Over the years, this diligent family of four built onto that yellow and black bus emblazoned on each side with "Mercer County Schools." First, a bathroom was added on, then a living addition, and eventually a small kitchen was built off the back as well as a deck and a makeshift front porch. Over time, much of the bus began to disappear—the flattened tires, the driver's seat with steering wheel, the fold-out entrance doors—until one day the family was left with an actual home that wasn't sitting up on blocks anymore.

About a block away, Maw Maw and Paw Paw's home seemed like the Ritz Carlton. With a full-sized kitchen and a semi-finished basement, they did pretty well for retired coal miners who lived a good part of their married years in a tent colony on coal company property. A certain amount of this good living came from Paw Paw getting the black lung from years of working in the mines. In the late sixties, Congress established a black lung benefits program to which Paw Paw promptly applied and promptly received a hefty six-figure lump payout. And typical of solid country people who came from nothin', both Maw Maw and Paw Paw went to their graves without spending so much as a dime on themselves.

But Maw Maw and Paw Paw still kept enough food around to feed the entire congregation of Greenview Methodist Church, and stashed it (just like their lump-sum payout) all over the house. With a basement filled wall to wall with home-canned vegetables and meats, few trips were ever made to the local grocery store. They were completely self-sufficient, with nearly all of the canned goodies coming from Paw Paw's vegetable garden. His garden was an impressive sight to behold. The neighbors marveled at this local wonder. As the garden was built on a 70-degree ridge, it was hard believe he could get anything to grow there with the constant mountain flooding from summer rains, but somehow that green thumb of his made it work. There it was—rows of green beans, heirloom tomatoes, sweet corn, mounds of crispy cabbages, and crunchy red radishes. It was a vegetarian's delight, less all the fatback it was cooked in.

When we'd visit in the summer, oftentimes I'd get to "sleep over" in Maw Maw's basement on the old rickety twin bed with its half-painted iron frame and "hot dog" mattress (you know, the kind of mattress that folds you up like a hot dog if you lie in the middle). But somehow, that bed was still comfortable—probably because Maw Maw always made it up with her handmade quilt and crisp, fresh sheets just before I came over.

No one had air-conditioning back then (and it could get quite warm in the summer), so a drafty basement with a cement floor was a welcome relief. Next door, at my Granny Boohler's house, every bed, couch, and available floor space was packed with aunts, uncles, and cousins from bottom to top, and even at the ripe old age of eleven, I think I needed some peace.

After dinner, Maw Maw would saunter down the creaky wood stairs and tuck me in, dressed in her characteristic oversized brown print smock, and softly uttering the same apologetic phrases, "Well honey, I knows you want to stay on up, but me and Paw Paw's tarred tonite—he's been pullin' weeds out der all day. Dontchu whirry. You can c'mon back tamara and slep ovah." I would hold onto those words like a fistful of diamonds just waiting for night to pass so I could start the process over again the next day. I just loved being there.

On some nights, when I couldn't sleep, Maw Maw would lie next to me in the adjoining twin bed and wait for me to fall asleep, which I rarely did. Instead, she would fall asleep on her back with legs gently crossed, her hands resting on her chest peacefully, and emitting just enough of a snore that I knew not to try and start up any conversation. She seemed old to me then, with her tightly wound silvery brown curls, deeply embedded facial lines, and skin heavily pigmented from too many long days in the sun.

In the middle of the night, when I'd wake up, Maw Maw would be gone. Feeling a little scared (being down there by myself now), for entertainment I'd count the Ball jars lined along with wall. They were always properly organized by their contents—eleven jars pickled wax beans, eight jars sweet corn, six jars pickled beets, ten jars apple butter, seven jars bread-and-butter pickles, four cans homemade sausage. I remember how the moonlight would creep in and bounce off the golden colors of the corn and the freshly packed cucumbers still glistening in their vinegar.

Immediately, I'd feel better as it reminded me of Maw Maw's cooking—the quintessential vegetable plate with fresh, sliced tomatoes, collard greens cooked in fatback, apple cider–laced cole slaw, and mushy butter beans. And sweets! Her sweet potato pie was pure heaven. Simply garnished with a dollop of fresh cream and a sprinkle of nutmeg, it was the perfect ending to the perfect meal.

Maw Maw passed away a few years ago, tipping the age scales at 103 years. After her funeral, friends and family gathered at the house, doing what we all do in the country when someone beloved passes on—bearing sweets. Although in Maw Maw's case, it may have seemed more appropriate to bring a couple of jars of homemade apple butter or canned cream corn, the people who loved her most brought gooey brownies, homemade cinnamon rolls, and apple date pies. There was, of course, a West Virginia Funeral Cake—a chocolate-cinnamon–infused cake with chocolate icing, which originated out of the coalfields. Made from ingredients on hand in every country cook's kitchen (flour, sugar, eggs, and chocolate) it is designed to be made at the last minute and leave a lasting impression. The West Virginia Funeral Cake's sole purpose is to brighten up even the saddest of days, and it truly does.

Every cookie, cake, and pie savored that day was made in Maw Maw's honor because in many ways, that's why we all cook—to give back to the people we love. The meals that Maw Maw cooked for me were fashioned out of love, and eating her food made me proud to be part of everything Mercer County, where a school bus can be a home or a particularly fruitful garden a symbol of community stature; where Ball jars and fresh vegetables are enough to live on, and six-figure lump payouts don't mean nothing next to the Bible.

Comforting Friends and Family

Make it chocolate. Chocolate always makes people feel better, and the West Virginia Funeral Cake has been known to lift even the darkest of spirits.

Make it unexpected. Pop by unannounced at the home of those in mourning with sweets in hand. We call it "receiving friends." Give a hug and leave your goodie. It's a great way to say all the right things without really saying anything at all.

Be prepared. Keep your pantry well stocked. Flour, sugar, shortening, evaporated milk, vanilla, and chopped nuts should always be on hand because you never know when the services of a freshly baked cinnamon roll will be required.

Bring on the church ladies. Call up one of your church ladies, announce the name of your deceased, and then sit back and watch piles upon piles of delicious home-cooked treats arrive at your door. But be prepared to reciprocate because church ladies never forget.

Feel free to dig in. There's no reason to feel guilty about eatin' up any funeral fixin's. Be the first one in line to slice into that untouched pie because, although you and the deceased may be in the same room, you're the one that's still alive.

MISS VIOLET'S CINNAMON ROLLS

1 recipe dough from Miss Violet's
  Potato Rolls (page 90)
$^1/_2$ cup brown sugar
2 teaspoons ground cinnamon

$^1/_2$ cup chopped pecans
2 tablespoons butter
1 cup powdered sugar
1 cup milk

Grease up a good-sized pan.

Roll out your dough into a 12 by 12-inch square. Mix up your sugar and cinnamon. Sprinkle this over the dough and do the same with the pecans. Dot some butter evenly over the dough. Roll up jelly roll style and cut in $^1/_2$-inch slices. (Miss Violet thinks dental floss works great for really clean cuts, and she oughta know since her husband was a dentist!)

Place the slices in the pan. Cover and let rise in a warm place until doubled in size, 90 minutes to 2 hours.

Turn on your oven to 375 degrees. Bake the rolls for 15 minutes. While they're baking, mix together the powdered sugar and milk to make a glaze. Take those rolls out of the oven and let 'em cool a bit, then drizzle with the glaze. Serve warm from the oven.

BROWNIE'S CHOCOLATE MINT SQUARES

These triple-layer chocolate bars filled with minty goodness are guaranteed to cheer up anybody who's feeling down. Make sure you keep 'em in the fridge since they're no good if they melt.

3 sticks plus 6 tablespoons butter,
   softened
1 cup white sugar
4 eggs, beaten
1 (16-ounce) bottle chocolate syrup
1 cup flour

1 teaspoon vanilla extract
2 cups powdered sugar, sifted
$1/4$ cup crème de menthe
   (fancy peppermint liqueur)
1 cup semisweet chocolate morsels

Turn on your oven to 350 degrees. Grease up and flour a 9 by 12-inch glass baking dish.

Cream up 2 sticks of the butter and the sugar until real light and fluffy. Toss in your eggs, chocolate syrup, flour, and vanilla. Pour into baking dish. Spread it up real evenly. Bake for about 30 minutes and let cool.

For your second layer, get out a big bowl and mix up your powdered sugar and 1 stick of butter. Add in your crème de menthe. Spread over your cooled cake.

For your top layer, get out your double boiler and melt your chocolate and the rest of the butter (or carefully set a glass bowl over simmering hot water to make a double boiler). Cool your chocolate mixture up and then spread over your Crème de Menthe layer. Now, go make someone happy.

FLOSSIE'S TEXAS TORNADO CAKE

$1^1/2$ cups white sugar
2 cups flour
2 tablespoons baking soda
Pinch of salt
2 eggs
2 cups canned fruit cocktail
   (with juice)

$1/2$ cup brown sugar
1 cup chopped walnuts
1 stick shortening (or butter)
$3/4$ cup sugar
$1/2$ cup evaporated milk
1 cup sweetened flaked coconut

Turn on your oven to 325 degrees. Grease up a 9 by 12-inch glass baking dish.

Sift up your sugar, flour, baking soda, and salt. Beat in your eggs, one at a time. Then, toss in your fruit cocktail. Mix it all really good. Pour into your baking dish. Take another bowl and mix together the brown sugar and walnuts. Sprinkle the walnut mixture over the cake batter. Bake for 40 to 45 minutes.

Boil your shortening, sugar, and milk in a pot for 2 minutes, stirring a lot. Add the coconut. Spoon this over your cake as soon as it comes outta the oven. Let your cake set a while before cuttin' into it.

MAW MAW'S WEST VIRGINIA FUNERAL CAKE

1 stick butter
1 cup sugar
1 egg, beaten
1 teaspoon vanilla extract
1 cup flour
2 tablespoons cocoa
$1/4$ teaspoon ground cinnamon
1 teaspoon baking soda
$1/4$ teaspoon ground cloves
1 cup buttermilk

FROSTING
1 stick butter, melted
$2/3$ cup unsweetened cocoa
3 cups powdered sugar
$1/3$ cup milk
1 teaspoon vanilla extract

Turn on your oven to 350 degrees. Lightly grease up a 9-inch square baking pan.

Cream up your butter and sugar until fluffy. Throw in the egg and vanilla. Mix and sift your dry ingredients and add this alternately with the buttermilk to the cream mixture. Stir until it's real smooth. Pour your batter into the pan and bake for 30 to 35 minutes.

To make the frosting, mix together your butter and cocoa in a big bowl. Alternately, add sifted powdered sugar and milk to the cocoa mixture, and beat it well, 'til you get a spreading consistency. Toss in your vanilla. Additional milk or sugar may be added if your frosting gets too thick. Spread it on your warm cake, and make sure to lick the spoon!

AUNT RUTHIE'S APPLE DATE PIE
BAKED IN A BROWN PAPER BAG

2 unbaked pie crusts (page 154)
4 cups peeled and diced apples
$1/2$ cup pitted and diced dates
$1/2$ cup quartered maraschino cherries
$1/2$ cup chopped walnuts

$3/4$ cup sugar
$1/4$ cup flour
$1/4$ teaspoon salt
$1/4$ cup light cream
$1/4$ cup lemon juice

Turn on your oven to 400 degrees.

Line up your pie pan with one of the pastries. Mix up your apples, dates, cherries, and nuts and put the mixture into your pie shell.

Mix up your sugar, flour, and salt. Pour in your cream and mix it all together real good. Add the lemon juice. Pour your cream mixture over your fruit. Make a fancy lattice design out of your other pastry by cutting it in strips and draping the strips over the pie.

Now, put your pie in a big brown paper bag. Close up your bag and fasten it tight (kitchen string works well for this). Bake up your pie for about 1 hour, or until it sets up. Remove the pie from the bag as soon as it comes out of the oven and let cool.

BESSIE JEAN'S YALLAR YAM PIE

Bessie Jean swears that it's the vanilla pudding mix that makes her sweet potato pie the absolute best. This pie is dense, rich, and sugary—everything a sweet potato pie should be. Serve with a big spoonful of freshly whipped cream and an extra sprinkle of nutmeg on top.

1 (12-ounce) can evaporated milk	1 cup brown sugar
1 cup milk	1 teaspoon ground nutmeg
2^1/$_2$ cups cooked, mashed sweet potatoes (fresh only, no canned!)	1 teaspoon vanilla extract
	2 teaspoons shortening, melted
1 (3-ounce) packet vanilla pudding mix	2 eggs, beaten
	2 unbaked pie crusts (page 154)

Turn on your oven to 450 degrees.

Toss all your ingredients in a blender and whip 'em up 'til smooth. Pour into pie shells and cover the edges of your pie with foil. Bake for 10 minutes. Then turn the oven down to 350 degrees and bake an additional 45 minutes to an hour, or until your pie is set up.

Ball Jar Baked Cake

Canned cakes make a tasty gift. Just bake your cake in a wide-mouth pint canning jar and seal as you would any other canned food.

What you'll need:
5 or 6 pint-sized wide-mouth canning jars
Shortening, to grease the jars
$1/2$ recipe Granny Boohler's West Virginia Applesauce Cake (page 70)
Fabric, trim, and ribbon (optional)

1. Sterilize the jars. Generously grease up the inside of the jar but not the rims.
2. Mix up your cake batter and pour exactly 1 cup into each jar.
3. Wipe the jar rims clean and place on a baking sheet. Bake for 45 minutes in a 325-degree oven. While your cake bakes, prepare your canning lids according to manufacturer's directions.
4. Take out your cakes and seal immediately with sterilized caps. As your cake cools, you should hear the lids "pop." Treat your cakes as you would any other canned good. If the seal is broken or your cake appears spoiled in any way, discard it. These cakes should last about 3 months.
5. For gifts, decorate your jar lids with leftover fancy fabrics, seasonal trim, and ribbons. Don't forget to attach a copy of the cake recipe to your jar, noting its shelf life.

Part Four

CREATIN' YOUR OWN GATHERIN' FROM SCRATCH

CREATIN'
YOUR OWN GATHERIN'
FROM SCRATCH

As a little girl, I just loved to flip through my mother's old cookbooks and read recipes. My mouth would water as I read each ingredient, envisioning how the sweet creaminess of a melting scoop of vanilla ice cream would taste combined with a forkful of lemony sponge cake. I simply adored perusing pages and pages of homespun recipes. While the rest of the kids in school were reading Judy Blume books, I was reading *Betty Crocker Cookbook* and *Joy of Cooking* from front to back. These cookbooks, along with others from the Mercer County Women's Club, Westbriar Baptist Church, and Allegheny Mountain Buttercup Garden Club, shaped me into the home chef I am today.

Along with reading, there was plenty of showing and telling in our family. I'd often sit in Granny's kitchen while she cooked, peeking over her shoulder from time to time just to see what in the world she was stirring in that big black pot. I'd watch how she cut biscuits without ever twisting the can or how she greased up her bundt pans with gobs of shortening before pouring in the cake batter. I learned so much from simply watching her.

I'd watch my mother cook, too. On certain Saturday afternoons, our house would be overrun with the smell of fresh, ripe peaches slowly cooking down into homemade jam. I'd watch her carefully remove each sterilized jar from a vat of boiling water, always thinking what a dangerous practice canning seemed to be. But she knew what she was doing, and it showed in the confidence of her actions. But the true joy was sampling a spoonful of that caramel-colored jam straight from the pot, which always seemed to burst with a perfect balance of sweet and tart.

Then there were the volumes of handwritten recipes that were literally strewn about our kitchen in drawers, magazine racks, shoe boxes, and bookcases. Every Christmas I'd find a handful of these precious recipes in my Christmas bucket. Our Christmas stockings were often lost in the attic somewhere, so after futilely searching for them, my mom would eventually put all my stocking treats in a big plastic bucket rescued from the basement. That bucket would hang from the tree right next to the forever chirping electric birdcage, and on Christmas morning I'd dig into it, trying to ignore the fact that it was probably used to mop the floor two days before. Yet, these Christmas bucket recipes served as little gems that had been passed down from my granny's granny, her granny's granny, and so on. After many Christmases, I had acquired quite the collection, and it wasn't long before I, too, was stashing these little strips of paper in boxes, folders, and drawers to save for my special gatherings.

The recipes included here in Part Four are a true cross-section of inspiration drawn from community cookbooks, Granny's recipes scribbled on scraps of paper, and pure observation. The recipes are divided into chapters, making selecting a particular appetizer, meat, or dessert for your next gathering a little easier. I hope that as you read through each ingredient and preparation, you can taste them, too, because all the recipes in this book are the best of the best from my quirky family to yours.

Recipe for Happiness

2 bushels of Understanding	1 pinch of Advice
1 peck of Compassion	$1/2$ dash of Criticism
6 pounds of Tenderness	A few drops of Tears
3 gallons of Kindness	A little bit of Sadness
4 bunches of Sweetness	

Mix together understanding, compassion, tenderness, and kindness. Add in big handfuls of sweetness and mix alternately with advice, criticism, tears, and sadness. (Do not overmix.) Finally, add your secret ingredient—Love—because without it, your Happiness will be not be complete.

Chapter 12

PICKIN' FROM THE RELISH TRAY

MAMA BAILEY'S PIMIENTO CHEESE SPREAD AND SALTINES

One of my all-time favorite Southern snacks is homemade pimiento cheese spread. The tang of the Colby cheese and cayenne pepper blends deliciously with the creaminess of the mayonnaise and cream cheese. Real homemade pimiento cheese is best stirred by hand so all the lumps and chunks are intact. Serve with salty crackers.

12 ounces Colby or a medium
sharp yellow cheese, grated

6 ounces cream cheese, softened

1/4 cup mayonnaise

1/4 teaspoon cayenne pepper

1 to 2 teaspoons pimiento juice

2 to 3 tablespoons diced pimiento, or to taste

Mix up your cheeses, mayonnaise, cayenne pepper, and pimiento juice. Stir in the pimientos by hand and put the mixture in the fridge to chill. It's best if it sets overnight. Mama Bailey swears that this is the best thing to take to a picnic.

DRUNKEN WEENIES

These little weenies really pack a whollop. Made with a good amount of bourbon, these little guys are as liquored up as you'll be after eatin 'em. (Caution: Keep away from children unless you want their game playing to consist of "Quarters" and "Keg Stands".)

1/2 cup bourbon

1 cup ketchup

1 cup brown sugar

Cocktail weenies

Mix all your ingredients in a pot and cook, uncovered, on low for 30 minutes. Transfer to your favorite crockpot and serve right outta the pot with toothpicks.

REMY AND MAX'S DRIED APPLE SNACKS

Make this recipe on a cold day to enjoy a nice, warm kitchen.

About 12 tart cooking apples, peeled and quartered
2 cups apple cider
$^1/_2$ cup honey (or use more or less, to taste)
45 cinnamon red hot candies (or use more or less, to taste)

Put your apples and cider in a big ole pot and bring up to a simmer. Stir every now and then so it doesn't stick. Cook your apples on low heat until you get a sort of watery apple butter. Then cool the mixture and throw it in your blender (if you have a fancy food processor, now's the time to pull that out). Mix it up good. Then throw it back in the pot and add your honey and candies. Cook until your mixture starts to look like thick apple butter.

Put some parchment paper on a baking sheet and spread out your apple mixture about $^1/_4$ inch thick. Then stick the mixture in the oven on real low heat (about 120 degrees) to dry it out. Keep the oven door just a bit ajar so all the moisture can escape. This will take about 14 hours.

Take it out of the oven, let it cool, and then peel it off the paper and roll up jelly roll style. Cut into slices. Store in a Ball jar.

HOTTIE'S BAKED CLAM DIP

1 (8-ounce) package cream
 cheese, softened
1 (6-ounce) can clams,
 well drained
2 tablespoons minced onion
1 tablespoon buttermilk

$^1/_2$ teaspoon prepared horseradish
$^1/_4$ teaspoon salt
Pinch of pepper
$^1/_3$ cup almonds, sliced and toasted
 in butter
Crackers, for serving

Turn on your oven to 375 degrees.

Mix up your cream cheese and clams with the rest of your ingredients (except for the almonds). Spoon the mixture into an ovenproof dish and sprinkle with the almonds.

Bake for 15 minutes. Serve with a pile of buttery crackers.

BIG BUTT BEA'S WHITE TRASH NACHOS

1/2 box buttery crackers
1/2 pound sharp Cheddar cheese,
   shredded (use more, if you like
   it cheesy)

1/2 pound bacon, cooked and crumbled
Pickled jalapeños (optional)
Sour cream, for serving
Salsa, for serving

Turn on your oven to about 400 degrees. Line up a casserole dish with buttery crackers. Sprinkle with some cheese. Top with crumbled bacon and jalapeños. Bake it all until your cheese is good and melted. Serve with sour cream and salsa. Play a little mariachi music in the background for added Mexican flavor.

DEVIL'S DELIGHT

Best make sure you make it to Sunday church service before you serve up this mischievous little appetizer. Made with a can of condensed soup blended with cream cheese, deviled ham, and onions, this wicked spread is fit for Beezlebub himself.

1 (8-ounce) package cream
   cheese, softened
1/2 of an 11-ounce can of condensed
   tomato soup
2 (4 1/2-ounce) cans deviled ham
1/4 cup minced cucumber

4 tablespoons minced green onion
1 small clove garlic, minced
Hot sauce, to taste
Salt and pepper, as much as you like
Potato chips or Melba toast

Beat your cream cheese with an electric mixer and then add the rest of your ingredients. Mix it up real good. Then put it in the fridge and set back and relax while it chills. Serve with chips or Melba toast.

Chapter 13

"REAL" SALADS

FOUR BOYS AND A SHOTGUN CORNBREAD SALAD

You can do a lot of stuff with cornbread. Stuff it in a glass of buttermilk (see page 27), panfry it in butter, mix it in a casserole, and even make a salad out of it. This is a great way to use up any leftover cornbread that has started to dry out.

DRESSING

2 cups mayonnaise

3 tablespoons pickle relish, plus a little juice

1 tablespoon apple cider vinegar

1 tablespoon sugar

2 teaspoons dry mustard

Salt and pepper, as much as you like

1 onion, chopped

1 green bell pepper, chopped

1 large tomato, chopped

About 12 slices bacon, cooked and crumbled

1 (8 by 8-inch) pan cornbread (can be made fresh from a mix if no leftover is available), crumbled into large chunks

First, make your dressing. Mix up your mayo, pickle relish (and juice), apple cider vinegar, sugar, and mustard. Season with salt and pepper the way you like it. Refrigerate until ready to use.

Next, in a big bowl, layer up your onions, bell peppers, tomatoes, bacon, and cornbread, and pour half of the dressing over it all. Start over again, but this time, add the cornbread first, then the onions, bell pepper, tomatoes, bacon, and dressing. Cover and refrigerate overnight. Toss a little just before serving.

BACON GREASE WILTED SALAD

Fry up enough bacon to get 2 to 3 tablespoons of bacon grease (6 to 8 slices). Save your bacon. Mix up your bacon grease with 2 to 3 tablespoons of vinegar and 1 to 2 tablespoons of sugar. Taste to get the sweetness you like. Your dressing should be tangy. Pour this mixture into a pan and bring it to a boil. Remove from the heat and put your salad together.

Tear up about 6 to 8 cups of leaf lettuce and chop 4 to 5 green onions, including the green tops. Pour the warm dressing over the salad and toss while it's all still warm. Add a little black pepper. Crumble some bacon on top and serve right away.

BABY NICKY FIVE-BEAN SALAD

1 can cut green beans, drained	1 large onion, sliced thin
1 can yellow wax beans, drained	$2/3$ cup sugar
1 can garbanzo beans, drained	$3/4$ cup wine vinegar
1 can black beans, rinsed and drained	$1/3$ cup vegetable oil
1 can kidney beans, rinsed and drained	1 teaspoon garlic salt
	1 teaspoon pepper
1 large green bell pepper, diced	Fresh chopped dill, as much as you like

Mix up your beans, green pepper, and onions in a large bowl. Mix the sugar, vinegar, oil, garlic salt, and pepper in a bowl and pour over the vegetables. Add the dill and toss gently to coat. Put in the fridge to chill for at least 24 hours. Stir your beans several times during the 24-hour period. This will keep in the refrigerator for a week to ten days and just keeps gettin' better over time.

NANNER FRUIT COCKTAIL

This ain't no cocktail hour drink. It is the easiest starter on the planet and makes a great dessert. We call it a "grease cutter" since you can sure bet the rest of the meal is gonna have some fat in it. Serve your cocktail in elegant martini glasses or dessert bowls and everyone will forget it came from a can.

Open a can of fruit cocktail and slice up a couple of bananas. Stir together and serve in your fanciest of dishes.

WEST VIRGINIA SALAD OIL

Most of the time, when I was growing up, the word "salad" referred to a shiny, congealed concoction of green gelatin, pineapple cubes, tiny marshmallows, and whipped cream. But there were times when we had just a regular ole iceberg-style salad, and this salad oil recipe was always served up alongside.

1 cup white vinegar	2 cups vegetable oil
2 cups sugar	Just under 1 tablespoon salt
1 cup ketchup	1 large onion, grated

Mix all of your ingredients in your blender. Serve up with your favorite veggies.

Chapter 14

KILLIN' AND GRILLIN'—
BEEF, PORK, AND GAME

LOU LOU'S FRIED SQUIRREL

After you shoot up a couple of tree rats, make sure to clean 'em real good. Then parboil your squirrels in a little salted water for about 20 minutes or so. Let 'em cool. Cut your squirrel into small serving pieces much like you would chicken. Flour your pieces good and sprinkle with salt and pepper the way you like it. Melt about a $1/4$ inch shortening in your cast iron skillet along with a little butter. When your grease gets good and hot, fry your squirrel pieces until they are nice and brown.

Lower your heat and add $1/4$ cup water to your skillet. Put on a tight-fitting lid and let your squirrel steam for another 20 minutes. Take off the lid and continue cooking until it gets a crispy coating and most of the liquid has evaporated. Lou Lou always said you gotta cook your squirrel a real long time to get all the squeal out of it. Take out your squirrel and drain it on a paper bag.

Make a gravy out of any liquid that's left in the pan by adding a little flour to your pan drippings. Slowly stir in some milk, 'til it gets nice and thick the way you like. Add salt and pepper the way you like it. Serve your squirrel and gravy over a big pile of home-made biscuits.

PORCUPINE BALLS

Whatever you do, don't confuse these beefy nuggets with mountain oysters. Mountain oysters, a.k.a. prairie oysters, swinging beef, or cowboy caviar, are bull testicles that are marinated, fried, or seared in a hot pan. They represent a fine white trash delicacy. Porcupine balls, on the other hand, while resembling the mountain oyster in nickname, are merely regular ole ground beef and rice meatballs. They get their name from the cooked rice that pokes out of the meatball, resembling the quills of a porcupine.

1^1/$_2$ pounds lean ground beef
^{1}/$_2$ cup raw long grain rice
1 small onion, chopped
^{1}/$_2$ cup milk
1 tablespoon horseradish
1 tablespoon Worcestershire sauce
1 clove garlic, minced
1 teaspoon Italian seasoning
1 teaspoon dried oregano
1 teaspoon salt
Pinch of celery salt
Pinch of pepper

SAUCE
1 (32-ounce) can diced tomatoes, drained
1 (15-ounce) can diced Southwestern spiced tomatoes or canned stewed tomatoes, drained
1 (16-ounce) can tomato juice
1 (10-ounce) can tomato soup
1 cup water
2 teaspoons Worcestershire sauce
2 teaspoons Italian seasoning
1 teaspoon dried oregano
1 tablespoon sugar

To make the balls, mix up all of the ingredients and gently form into balls about the size of small hen eggs. Brown your balls on all sides in a little hot oil in a deep pan and leave them in the pan.

To make your sauce, mix all of the ingredients in a big bowl. Add this to the pan with the balls, cover, and simmer for about 1 hour, or until the rice is tender and your gravy starts to get thick. Add a little more tomato juice and water if your gravy gets too thick.

BEEF ROAST "ALL BURNT UP" WITH VEGGIES

My Granny Boohler was renowned for burning up dinner. As someone who loved to spend hours chatting on the phone, Granny would be so wrapped up in a tall tale that she would sometimes forget her roast in the oven. "It's just a little beyond golden brown," she would say, as she unveiled the roast in all its black-encrusted glory. But it was that blackened crust that ended up making her roasts so darn good.

2-inch cut of sirloin beef roast
   (large enough for your crowd and enough for leftovers)
Plenty of shortening
Enough potatoes, onions, and carrots for your crowd

Put enough shortening in a deep cast iron pan to cover the bottom and be a good $1/4$ inch deep when melted. Heat grease to almost smoking and add beef. Watch out—it'll splatter.

Brown your beef well on both sides, then stand it up on its edges and brown them, too. Cook until about half done on the inside. Then add about a half cup or more of water, put on a tight-fitting lid, and turn down the heat to low. When the meat is tender, remove the lid and turn up the heat to about medium-high to recrisp your meat on all sides. Remove the meat and put it on a big ole plate.

Peel your potatoes, onions, and carrots and cut them into large chunks about the size of small hen eggs. Add these veggies to the same hot greased-up pan and cover with 1 to 2 cups of water. Cook until tender. Salt and pepper the way you like it.

Add your veggies to the plate with your meat and pour the pan juices over. Keep your leftovers for your Second-Day Dinner (facing page).

SECOND-DAY DINNER—"ALL BURNT UP" BEEF ROAST WITH BROWN GRAVY

Take your leftover roast and slice it into real thin pieces. Heat up a little leftover grease and brown your beef slices real good. Turn the heat down and sprinkle 2 to 3 tablespoons of flour over the beef. Stir to brown your flour real good. Now, add some milk (at least a cup and a half) using half evaporated milk and half regular milk. Add a little at a time, and stir quickly with a wooden spoon to get the lumps out. If it's too thick, just add some water, but remember, as it cools it gets thicker. It will take lots of salt and pepper to flavor it right, so just keep adding and tasting. Serve beef gravy over homemade buttermilk biscuits (page 52).

12-POINT BUCK VENISON ROAST

4 pounds venison rump roast	1 large onion, sliced
Salt and pepper, as much as you like	2 (12-ounce) cans of beer
2 tablespoons Italian seasoning	1 (16-ounce) jar spicy peppers in tomato sauce

Remove all fat and gristle from your deer roast. Stick your roast in a large, deep pan. Season well with salt and pepper and then rub Italian seasoning into meat. Cover with sliced onions. Pour both cans of beer over the meat. Cover with foil and place in the refrigerator overnight.

Next day, put your roast and the marinade and onions into a big ole crockpot. Stir your spicy peppers into the marinade. Cover the crockpot and cook on low heat for 7 to 9 hours, or until your rump roast is tender and falling off the bone. Serve up your roast with a couple of cans of cheap beer.

CHUBBY HUBBY MEATLOAF

SAUCE

1/2 small onion, minced

1 tablespoon vegetable oil

2 small garlic cloves, minced

1 cup ketchup

1 tablespoon apple cider vinegar

1 teaspoon soy sauce

2 teaspoons Worcestershire sauce

1/4 cup brown sugar

1 teaspoon chile powder

2 teaspoons hot sauce (optional)

Salt and pepper,
   as much as you like

1 onion, diced

1 green bell pepper, diced

1/2 cup diced celery

1 1/2 pounds lean ground beef
   or prepared meatloaf mixture

3/4 cup uncooked oats

1/2 cup buttermilk

2 eggs, beaten

1 1/2 tablespoons horseradish

1 tablespoon Worcestershire sauce

1 teaspoon salt

1/2 teaspoon pepper

First you gotta make your sauce. Sauté your onion in the vegetable oil. Once it's good and soft, add your garlic, but be careful not to burn it. Add the rest of your ingredients for the sauce except for the salt and pepper and cook, uncovered, on medium-low for 15 to 20 minutes, or until your flavors come together. Season with salt and pepper the way you like it.

Turn on your oven to 375 degrees.

Now, heat up a big pan. Add some shortening to the hot pan, and then add your onion, green pepper, and celery and toss 'em around, cooking until they get soft. Set aside in a bowl. In a separate bowl, mix up the rest of the ingredients and stir in 1/4 cup of the BBQ sauce you just made. Add your cooked vegetables and lightly mix everything up with your hands. Gently form into an oval loaf in a shallow baking dish. Spread the top with the rest of the BBQ sauce (save a little to serve on the side). Bake for about 1 hour. Make sure to save up your leftovers for sandwiches.

CHARLIEKIN'S CORN DOGS

To help your batter stick to your weenie while it is being fried, you gotta first make sure your weenies are at room temperature. Then dry them real good with a paper towel and dust each weenie with flour before dipping and frying. You will need 8 popsicle sticks to make these.

2/3 cup cornmeal	1/2 cup milk
1/3 cup all-purpose flour	2 tablespoons oil
1 tablespoon sugar	8 weenies
1 teaspoon salt	Peanut oil, for frying
1 egg	Mustard or a favorite dipping sauce, for serving

Mix up your dry ingredients in a bowl. In another bowl, beat the egg with the milk and oil and add to the dry ingredients. Skewer your weenies with popsicle sticks. Dip each one into the batter and coat it completely. Heat up some peanut oil to very hot, about 375 degrees, and put the weenies into it, cooking them until they turn a nice golden brown. Drain on paper towels and serve immediately with your favorite mustard or dipping sauce.

POOL ROOM HOT DOG CHILI

West Virginians are dead serious about their hot dogs and their homemade hot dog chili. Nearly everyone has their own secret recipe. This one is from our family and, unlike most hot dog chilis, is made without tomato sauce or ketchup. Make yourself up a slaw dog with an all-beef hot dog topped with this chili. Then slather it in Burris Honeycutt's Cider Slaw (page 90). Enjoy your hot dog in a smoky pool room with a really big beer.

$1/4$ cup shortening

4 tablespoons diced onions

3 cloves garlic, minced

3 pounds lean ground beef

$1^1/2$ tablespoons chile powder

1 teaspoon cayenne pepper

1 tablespoon ground cumin

1 tablespoon black pepper

1 tablespoon salt

$1^1/2$ teaspoons paprika

$1/4$ teaspoon ground cinnamon

1 cup water plus 1 quart hot water

Get out your cast iron skillet and melt the shortening. Sauté up your onions and garlic. Add your beef and break it up into little pieces. Add in your spices and the cup of water and stir it around. Pour your chili into a crockpot and add the hot water. Cook on high for the first hour and then turn down the heat to low and let the chili cook for about 6 to 8 hours. Freezes well.

CAST IRON CUBE STEAK WITH CRISPY GRAVY

This is true comfort food with no holds barred. Grab yourself a can of pork 'n' beans (you don't even need to heat them) and a bowl of fried apples (page 22) to round out this meal. Sauce your steak with the "crispy nectar of the gods," and before you know it, you'll be pickin' the banjo after dinner.

<table>
<tr><td>¹/₂ cup shortening</td><td>1 cup milk</td></tr>
<tr><td>¹/₂ to 1 pound cube steak,
   cut into palm-sized pieces</td><td>1 (5-ounce) can evaporated milk</td></tr>
<tr><td>About 1 cup flour</td><td>1 teaspoon salt</td></tr>
<tr><td></td><td>1 teaspoon pepper</td></tr>
</table>

Heat up your cast iron pan to medium high. Add enough shortening (about ¹/₄ inch) to cover the bottom of your sizzling-hot pan. Roll the pieces of cube steak thoroughly on both sides in flour. The more flour the better because this is where your "crispies" come from.

Add your floured pieces to your pan, which will be close to smokin'. The steak pieces should brown quickly in the hot grease. Next, brown the other side and remove the steaks. Drain on paper towels and salt lightly.

You now have lots of crispy, brown flour leavin's in your fry pan. You may need to add a tablespoon or so of shortening to make enough grease for the gravy. Add 2 heaping tablespoons of flour to the grease and crispies. Stir it 'til it takes on a brown color. Turn down the heat to medium-low and slowly stir in your milk and then the evaporated milk, salt, and pepper. Carefully stir until gravy begins to thicken.

You are now ready to enjoy some golden brown cube steak topped with a little "crispy nectar of the gods."

PEARLIE'S HAWAIIAN TROPICS SPARERIBS

These ribs are so good that after just one you'll be dancing the huli huli. And after eating two, who knows what you'll do?

5 pounds spareribs
Salt and pepper, as much as you like
Dried onion powder
Dried garlic powder

SAUCE
4 cloves garlic, minced
1 tablespoon peeled and minced fresh ginger
$1/2$ cup brown sugar
$1/2$ cup soy sauce
$1^1/2$ cups ketchup
1 tablespoon brown mustard
$1/3$ cup oyster sauce
$1/2$ tablespoon hot chile sauce (or more if you like it spicy!)
$1/3$ cup minced green onions

Rub up your ribs with a little salt, pepper, dried onion, and powdered garlic. Let 'em set in the fridge overnight if you've got the time.

Turn on your oven to 275 degrees. Put the ribs on a baking sheet and cover tightly with foil. Bake until fork tender (about 2 to 3 hours). Practice your hula dancing while you wait for your ribs to cook.

Mix up all the ingredients for your sauce in a pan and cook, uncovered, for about 20 minutes. Heat up your grill. Toss your ribs on a hot grill and brush with the sauce. Cook 'em until they get a little crusty on the outside. Serve up with the extra sauce and a big pile of napkins.

Chapter 15

CHICKEN, TURKEY, LITTLE BIRDS, AND OTHER FAIR-FEATHERED FRIENDS

MOUNTAIN STATE CHICKEN AND DUMPLIN'S

The first thing you gotta do before makin' these chicken and dumplin's is kill yourself a big, fat hen. My Grandpa Woody used to kill our hens with his bare hands. He'd chase one down, wring its neck, and then pluck it clean for dinner. If you don't feel quite up to that yourself, you can always buy a whole roaster at the grocery store. For the dumplin's, it's easy enough to use a commercial biscuit mix. Just follow the directions on the package for making dumplin's. The key to light dumplin's is not to overwork them.

1 whole roasting hen, cleaned	1 can creamed chicken soup,
4 cups water	plus more as needed
2 cups chicken broth,	2 tablespoons butter
plus more as needed	Dumplin's
2 teaspoons salt	Fresh parsley, for garnish (optional)

Put your chicken, water, broth, and salt in a heavy-bottomed pot with a lid. Bring up to a boil and then turn down the heat some and let it simmer. Cook your hen 'til she's tender and falling off the bone.

Remove the chicken and put it in a dish to cool. Throw away any fat or skin and bone the chicken. Then cut it up into smaller pieces and set it aside. Add the bones back to the broth and simmer for 1 to $1^1/_2$ hours.

Remove the bones and strain your broth to get rid of any foam or bits of fat. Add the creamed chicken soup and butter to the strained liquid. You will need plenty of rich broth to cook your dumplin's. Add additional chicken broth and another can of soup if need be, for richness. Simmer for about 30 minutes. Return your cooked chicken pieces to the pot and drop your dumplin's in by the spoonful to cook in the hot broth. Season with salt and pepper the way you like it. Serve hot in a big ole bowl with a garnish of fresh parsley.

BAM BAM'S FANCY
APPLE BUTTER–GLAZED GAME HENS

2 whole Cornish game hens,
  rinsed and dried

Vegetable oil

Salt and pepper, as much as you like

2 tablespoons butter,
  cut into small pieces

$^1/_2$ cup apple butter (page 7)

1 tablespoon honey

1 tablespoon apple cider vinegar

1 tablespoon minced fresh sage leaves

$^1/_2$ teaspoon ground cinnamon

$^1/_2$ teaspoon ground ginger

Turn on your oven to 400 degrees.

Brush up your hens with vegetable oil and season with salt and pepper the way you like it. Stuff the butter pieces up under the skin of your birds. Make sure you get salt and pepper up into the hen's insides.

Get out a saucepan and throw in your apple butter, honey, and vinegar. Bring it up to a low simmer. Toss in your sage, cinnamon, and ginger and stir well.

Cook your hens for about 20 minutes. Remove from the oven and brush 'em up with your apple butter mixture. Put your hens back in the oven and let 'em roast for another 15 to 20 minutes, or until the juices run clear. If you get bored, for entertainment brush your hens with any leftover sauce as they cook.

CARETTA'S SHERRIED CHICKEN LIVERS

1 pound chicken livers

Milk

$^1/_4$ cup flour

Salt and pepper, as much as you like

3 tablespoons butter

$^1/_4$ cup minced onion

$^1/_2$ pound mushrooms, sliced

3 tablespoons Worcestershire sauce

2 tablespoons sherry

Minced fresh parsley, for garnish

Toasted bread, for serving

Soak your livers in milk overnight to get the weird taste out. Discard the milk.

In a brown paper bag, mix up your flour with some salt and pepper. Drain your livers and add to bag. Shake 'em up real good. Add butter to a cast iron fry pan and throw in your onion. Next, add your livers. Brown them real good. Once they're brown, add your mushrooms, Worcestershire sauce, and sherry. Cook for another 5 minutes, or until your mushrooms are cooked. Then take the pan off the heat and top with parsley. Serve hot with toasted bread.

WHITE TRASH CORDON BLEU

4 to 6 chicken breasts, boned

Diced cooked ham and
   Cheddar cheese

2 eggs, beaten

2 cups milk

Salt and pepper, as much as you like

2 cups cracker crumbs, crushed

Take your chicken breasts and split 'em open, but don't cut all the way through. Fill up the breasts with ham and cheese.

Whip up your beaten eggs, milk, and salt and pepper in a large bowl. In another bowl, smash your crackers. Dip the breasts in the egg mixture and then roll in the cracker crumbs.

Turn on your oven to 375 degrees.

Heat your skillet to medium-high and add about an inch of vegetable oil. Fry up your breasts until they are crispy good. Then put 'em on a baking sheet and bake 'til they're done, about 10 minutes. (Use your fancy oven thermometer to test for doneness and make sure it reads 170 degrees.) Serve 'em up hot and crispy on the outside.

FOO'S CHICKEN CHOW MEIN

SAUCE

$^1/_4$ cup cold water

1 tablespoon cornstarch

1 tablespoon soy sauce

1 tablespoon dry sherry

1 tablespoon sugar

Black pepper

$^1/_4$ cup vegetable oil

1 teaspoon sesame oil

1 cup cubed chicken

1 cup diced onion

2 tablespoons minced garlic

1 tablespoon minced fresh ginger

1 cup diced celery

2 cups bean sprouts

1 cup chicken stock

Chow mein noodles, for garnish

Cooked white rice, for serving

First, mix up your sauce. Combine the cold water and cornstarch and mix until well blended. Add your soy sauce, sherry, sugar, and as much black pepper as you like. Set aside.

Get out your big wok (or cast iron pan). Heat it up 'til it's real hot. Then add your oils and when they're close to smokin', add your chicken. Stir it around. Next up, add your onion, garlic, ginger, and celery (be careful not to burn your garlic) and cook it for a couple of minutes. Add your bean sprouts and your chicken stock and cook for 1 minute. Last, stir in your sauce mixture and bring up to a boil. Adjust the heat to medium-low and simmer until thick, about 3 more minutes. Serve over a steaming mound of white rice and top with crunchy chow mein noodles.

COUSIN BRAD'S FAVORITE TURKEY SAMMY

It's a general consensus that one of the best parts of Christmas is getting to eat all that leftover turkey. My cousin Brad showed me the light when it came to making the perfect leftover turkey sandwich. The recipe could not be simpler, and its simplicity is what makes it so darn good.

2 slices really soft, cheapo white bread
Thick slices of cold, leftover turkey breast
A good slathering of mayonnaise (preferably Hellman's)
Black pepper

Take your bread and slather it really good with lots of mayo. Lay a couple of slices of turkey breast down and sprinkle with black pepper. Press sandwich together and eat. To be more like my cousin Brad, eat more than one.

Chapter 16

HEADIN' DOWN TO
GRANDDADDY'S FISHIN' HOLE

My Granddaddy Belcher was a devoted freshwater fisherman. He'd often head out to the old dam and fish for trout, bass, or perch using his homemade lures and jigs. Sometimes he'd pull out a chartreuse broken minnow, other times he'd go for his silver spinner, and if he was really feeling it, he'd get out his fly rod and tie on a couple of hand-strewn flies and spend the rest of the afternoon casting away in the sun. Yet, he rarely brought any fish home. His moments down by the dam were all his, and I figure he could've cared less about actually hooking a fish. For him, it was all about the action—a toss here and a floating bobber there was all he needed to make the day worthwhile.

Shortly before he died, Granddaddy Belcher passed on his tackle box of lures to me. Every lure was made by hand, from the tightly woven flies to the silvery round lead heads carefully glued with sprouting plumages of pink feathers. Each lure was ordered by color and function—the orange plastic worms were in one section while the red surface poppers rested in another. It was his artwork. He could find beauty anywhere, even in the painted eyes of a chrome-colored insect.

Sometimes I'll take his tackle box and old fishing rod down to the river for a little tossing and bobbing myself. I'll cast out a few times, watching the river swirl by in unaffected movements. And for a moment, I'll become him, waiting for that little nibble or gentle tug. And when it comes, I'll just sit quietly until it passes because I never catch any fish either.

GOLDEN-CRUSTED QUICK-FRY FLOUNDER WITH CORN MINICAKES

This type of frying works well for most any fish, but it is other-worldly for fresh flounder. Serve up your fish with a hot baked potato, a bowl of vinegary cole slaw, and, of course, a pot of fresh-brewed sweet tea. And don't forget your corn minicakes—a great way to use up any leftover batter. Country folk love their cornmeal and they don't like wastin' it.

$1/2$ cup white stoneground cornmeal

$1/3$ cup yellow self-rising cornbread mix

Pinch of salt

$3/4$ cup milk, plus a little more for the corn minicakes (or use a little buttermilk)

1 pound of fresh flounder, catfish, or other white-fleshed fish

Pinch of baking soda, for the corn minicakes

Pinch of sugar, for the corn minicakes

Put your fry pan on medium-high heat. Add about a $1/4$ inch of (melted) shortening into your pan. Mix up your white cornmeal and yellow cornbread mix in a flat-bottomed bowl. Toss in a pinch or two of salt. Pour the milk into another shallow pan. Put your flounder in the milk, cover it well, and let it soak a minute. Then roll each piece of flounder in the cornmeal mixture and place, skin side down, in your fry pan. Cook until golden brown on the skin side and repeat on the other side. Once cooked, set aside on paper towels and salt lightly.

You should have about $1/2$ cup of meal left in your bowl after doing the fish. Add a generous pinch of baking soda, a pinch of sugar, and a pinch of salt to the meal and enough milk or buttermilk to make a soft, thick batter. Mix it up good. Then drop your minicake batter (about 1 tablespoon each) in alongside the frying fish. You should have 4 to 6 wafer-sized crusty corn morsels. Take 'em out when they're browned up and drain 'em on a paper towel before serving.

FERNIE'S OYSTER STEW

This stew is a great winter warm-up. Just dig out that old soup tureen you haven't used in a decade, light up a fire in your cast iron stove, and have a couple of friends over to enjoy this hearty stew with a side of homemade spoonbread (page 141). You can use either shallots (fancy garlicky tastin' onions) or red onions for this recipe.

$1/2$ stick butter	Dash of Worcestershire sauce
2 tablespoons minced shallots or red onions	1 pint oysters, plus oyster liquor
	Dash of hot sauce
1 tablespoon or more flour (depending how thick your want your stew)	Salt and pepper, as much as you like
	Crumbled cooked bacon, for garnish
2 small (5-ounce) cans evaporated milk	Minced green onion, for garnish
$2^1/2$ cups milk	Oyster crackers

Melt your butter in a large pot. Toss in your shallots and sauté until they're good and tender. Sprinkle your flour over and cook a few minutes (do not brown). Add evaporated milk, regular milk, and Worcestershire sauce. Heat to a low boil, or until your soup begins to thicken a bit. Last, add in your oysters and their liquor and cook just 'til your oysters begin to curl. Never overcook an oyster! Add in a little hot sauce and salt and pepper the way you like it. Take your stew off the heat and serve it up in big bowls, topped with bacon, green onions, and, of course, oyster crackers.

ROWENA'S FANCY BAKED TROUT WITH HERBS

2 whole trout, heads and all	Butter
Salt and pepper, as much as you like	Fresh herbs, such as rosemary,
Sliced lemons	thyme, parsley, and dill
Sliced Vidalia onions	Olive oil

Turn on your oven to 350 degrees. Grease up a casserole dish.

After you catch your fish, make sure its cavity is cleaned out of any fish guts or other yucky stuff. Season the inside well with salt and pepper and then stuff with lemon slices, onion slices, big pats of butter, and herbs of choice. Season the outside of your fish with more salt and pepper and then drizzle it with a little olive oil.

Place your fish in the casserole dish and cover tightly with foil. Bake until the fish is done and flakes easily with a fork, 15 to 20 minutes.

PATTY'S SALMON PATTIES

Fancy seafood like jumbo lump crabmeat is hard come by in the hills, so canned seafoods are often used in place of fresh. This is my mama's take on the crabless crab cake—the canned salmon cake. Made with bones and all, these little fried cakes may make you forget that "jumbo lump" even exists.

1 (15-ounce) can pink salmon
2 tablespoons apple cider vinegar
1 egg
1 onion, finely chopped
1 to 1¹/₂ cups crackers
  and breadcrumbs, mixed

2 tablespoons chopped pimiento
Dash of horseradish
Salt and pepper, as much as you like
¹/₄ cup shortening

Remove any dark skin from the salmon and put the salmon, juice, and bones (leave the bones out if you are squeamish) into a large bowl. Sprinkle with the cider vinegar to take away the fishy taste. Add egg, onion, crumbs, pimiento, horseradish, and salt and pepper the way you like it. Mix lightly and form into 6 or 7 patties. For more tender cakes, barely press everything together when forming.

Get your cast iron pan nice and hot. Add your shortening and fry your cakes until brown on both sides.

Patty's Salmon Patties make a great second-day lunch. Simply place a cold patty on a plain ole hamburger bun. Add lettuce, tomato, and mayo.

CECILIA'S SHRIMP CREOLE

Shrimp is about as hard to find in the hills as crab, but when we get a hold of it, it is a special night indeed. Using the classic "holy trinity" of aromatic seasonings, this Louisiana-style shrimp dish will make you feel like you're floating down the bayou on a warm summer night.

1/2 cup chopped onion
1/2 cup chopped celery
4 cloves garlic, chopped
3 tablespoons shortening
1 (16-ounce) can chopped tomatoes
1 (8-ounce) can tomato sauce
1/2 teaspoon salt

1 teaspoon sugar
1 teaspoon Worcestershire sauce
1/2 teaspoon chile powder
1 dash hot sauce, or more as needed
12 ounces medium-sized shrimp, peeled
   and deveined
1/2 cup chopped green bell pepper
Steamed white rice, for serving

In a deep cast iron pan, brown up your onion, celery, and garlic in shortening. Throw in the rest of your ingredients except for the shrimp and bell pepper and simmer for 45 minutes. Add the shrimp and bell pepper and cook for 5 to 7 minutes, or until the shrimp are pink. Add more hot sauce if you think you need it. Serve over a big pile of steamy white rice.

Chapter 17

VEGGIE PICKIN'S AND CANNIN'

MAW MAW'S BREAD-AND-BUTTER PICKLES

There ain't no bread and there ain't no butter in these deliciously sweet and pungent home-canned pickles, which are a staple on any relish tray. Serve 'em up with a big slice of Jeffro's Oatmeal Molasses Bread (page 143) garnished with a spread of butter and you've got yourself quite a relish plate.

6 to 7 pounds cucumbers, thinly sliced

2 red bell peppers, chopped

1 green bell pepper, chopped

$2^1/2$ to 3 pounds white onions, thinly sliced

4 cloves garlic, halved

$^1/3$ cup pickling or table salt (you can buy pickling salt at any major grocery store)

4 cups sugar

3 cups apple cider vinegar

2 tablespoons mustard seed

1 teaspoon turmeric

$1^1/2$ teaspoons celery seed

Have 8 pint or 4 quart canning jars sterilized and ready.

Toss up your cucumbers, sweet peppers, onions, garlic, and salt in a big bowl and cover with cold water. Refrigerate for 5 to 6 hours.

Drain off your water and discard garlic. In a large pot, bring up the rest of your ingredients to a boil. Add the cucumber mixture. Return everything to a boil and immediately take the pan off the heat. While it's still really hot, pack into sterilized canning jars leaving about $^1/2$ inch headspace. Remove air bubbles. Wipe jar rims and seal at once according to canning lid manufacturer's directions.

SURRENDA LEE'S PEACH JAM

Go down to the market and buy yourself a big bag of peaches. Make sure your peaches are real ripe. Peel and pit your peaches and then cut 'em up into small chunks. Get out your potato masher and lightly mash 'em, leaving plenty of peach chunks.

Now, get out your pot and simmer the peaches for about 15 minutes. Then measure out the peaches and pulp you have. For every 3 cups of peaches, use 2 cups of sugar. Add in your sugar and turn your heat up to medium, stirring a lot so your peaches don't stick. Cook until your mixture starts to thicken up. Your jam should be runny, but still a bit thick. Pour into sterilized jars and seal 'em up good according to canning lid manufacturer's directions.

Serve up your jam on biscuits, homemade rolls, or corn muffins.

THORNEY'S BLACK RASPBERRY JAM

If you look real hard you just might be able to find a mess of black raspberries growing alongside the road. But be careful when you pick 'em, 'cuz the snakes love 'em, too! You'll find pectin sold in the canning section in grocery stores.

1 package liquid or powdered pectin
4 to 5 cups black raspberries
6 to 7 cups sugar
6 to 7 (^{1}/2-pint) canning jars with lids

Follow the directions found on your package of pectin. You should end up with cooked jam that has the consistency of flowing lava, but remember, it thickens as it cools. Your jam should be a tad runny when you serve it up, so if it's too thick, just add a little water or apple or grape juice to thin it out. Store in sealed, sterilized jars.

REBA MAY'S CREAMY MASHED POTATOES

Peel and cut enough potatoes into chunks for your group. (I always make a little extra, so there will be leftovers for next-day tater cakes.) Cover your potatoes with water and cook until tender. Save your potato water to use when mashing.

Heat your mashing liquid, which should be half evaporated milk, half potato water, and a big chunk of butter. Using your potato masher (no electric mixers!), smash the potatoes and add enough hot liquid to make them fluffy. Add salt and pepper the way you like it. Pile the potatoes in a big bowl and make a well in the top of your potato mound. Add a generous spoonful of butter into your potato well while your potatoes are good and hot. Let it run down the sides like a tasty, buttery volcano.

REBA MAY'S NEXT-DAY FRIED TATER CAKES

Take your cold leftover mashed potatoes and shape 'em into half-inch-thick cakes about the size of a Ball canning jar lid. Dip both sides of the cakes lightly in flour. Fry over medium heat in shortening in a cast iron fry pan 'til both sides are browned and crispy. (Cast iron fries up the best cakes.) Season with salt and pepper the way you like it.

FRESH SHELLED BUTTER BEANS

It will take about 3 pounds of butter (also known as lima) beans in their shells to serve 4 to 6 hearty eaters. Shell up your beans and wash 'em well. Put the beans in a big pot with a lid and add as little water as possible to cook. Adding a level teaspoon of sugar along with salt and pepper will sweeten the pot. Cook on low for about 15 minutes, or just until tender. Do not overcook or they'll get all mushy. You want them to still be a little crunchy for second-day eating. Just reheat and serve.

"REAL" KUNTRY GRITS

There just ain't nothing like a hefty bowl of stoneground grits. This recipe is super simple, and is a great addition to a hearty breakfast of eggs, bacon, sausage, and biscuits. It's also an alternative to the slow-cooking method of watching and stirring your grits on the stove, which can take up to an hour. This takes under 20 minutes in all.

$1/2$ rounded cup plain white stoneground grits

2 cups water

$1/2$ teaspoon salt

Black pepper

Butter

Get out a microwavable bowl that is big enough to avoid boiling over and spattering your oven. Mix up your grits, water, and salt and stick in the microwave, uncovered. Cook on high for 4 minutes and then give it a good stir. Do this two more times, cooking 4 minutes and stirring after each cooking. Cook a final 3 minutes and then cool for at least 5 minutes before diving in. Sprinkle up your grits with lots of black pepper and as much butter as you can stand to eat.

HALE AVENUE CORN PUDDING

2 tablespoons butter, melted

$1^1/2$ cups evaporated milk

$1/4$ cup flour

$1/4$ cup sugar

$3/4$ teaspoon salt

$1/4$ teaspoon ground nutmeg

1 teaspoon vanilla extract

1 (15-ounce) can corn, drained

1 (15-ounce) can cream-style corn

2 eggs, beaten slightly

Turn on your oven to 350 degrees. Grease up an 8 by 8-inch baking dish with a little of your melted butter.

Combine your milk, flour, sugar, salt, nutmeg, and vanilla and whisk good to remove lumps. Stir in the rest of the ingredients, including the rest of your butter. Bake for 45 to 55 minutes, or until the center is set and the top is lightly browned.

WILD BILL JONES'S FRIED CABBAGE

Pick yourself out a big ole head of fresh cabbage. Be certain that it is solid and doesn't have worm holes in it. Fry up some bacon in a big pan, saving the grease. Cut your cabbage into 1-inch chunks or however big you like it. Put a couple of tablespoons of your bacon grease into an iron skillet or a heavy-bottomed pan. When the grease is hot, start adding the cabbage and stir to keep it from burning. You'll start out with a lot of cabbage, but it will cook down. Cook until the cabbage is tender and most of the water has evaporated. Add salt and pepper the way you like it and a little sugar if you want a sweet touch. Wild Bill likes to add a little cayenne to his for extra zip. Crumble the bacon on top and serve it up.

PUCKER'S PICKLED BEETS

There's no need to fear the pickled beet. Once you see how tasty these little guys are you'll be whipping 'em up on a routine basis. Don't forget to save any leftover beet juice to make up a batch of pickled eggs. Just boil and peel your eggs, drop 'em into a jar of pickled beet juice, and set 'em in the refrigerator overnight. Then enjoy your pink-colored eggs the next day.

1 can small whole or sliced beets
$1/2$ cup white sugar
$1/2$ cup brown sugar

$1/2$ cup apple cider vinegar
1 tablespoon pure maple syrup
Pinch of allspice

Drain the beets and save their juice. Put the beet juice, sugars, vinegar, syrup, and allspice in a small pan. Simmer on low heat for about 5 minutes. Put the beets into a quart jar and pour in the warm liquid. Cap the jar and store in the refrigerator for at least 24 hours before serving.

Chapter 18

SOUPS, BEANS, BREADS, AND CASSEROLES— HOW A CAN OF SOUP CAN LEAD TO INSTANT CULINARY GENIUS

GENIUS IN A DISH

At some point during the week in our house there was always some version of a casserole on the dinner table. Whether the accenting ingredient was a can of mushroom soup, a pound of Velveeta cheese, or box of Ritz crackers, the casserole was still one of the fastest, cheapest, and easiest meals we could make. Casseroles are a great way to use up any leftovers you have in the fridge since just about any combination will work. Don't toss out those leftover mashed potatoes, just layer them up with some of that ground beef you used for tacos the previous night and a bag of preshredded cheese. Now all you have to do is get out that bag of half-stale corn chips, sprinkle them on top, and toss the whole shebang in the oven. Nothing wasted, everything gained.

1 pound ground beef,
   browned and drained
$1/2$ cup chopped onion
2 (15-ounce) cans mixed
   vegetables, drained
1 can cream of celery soup

1 teaspoon dried oregano
1 teaspoon dried basil
Salt and pepper, as much as you like
3 cups mashed potatoes (page 133)
Butter
1 cup shredded Cheddar cheese

Turn on your oven to 375 degrees.

Put your ground beef and onion in a large casserole dish. Add canned vegetables, soup, oregano, basil, and salt and pepper the way you like it. Mix it up well. Spread mashed potatoes on top, dot with bits of butter, and sprinkle with cheese. Bake in the oven for 30 to 45 minutes, or until bubbly.

JUANITA'S MEXICAN CASSEROLE

This is about as close as anyone in my family has gotten to south of the border, unless you count Pedro's rest stop, which divides North Carolina from South Carolina.

1 pound hot sausage	1 tablespoon chile powder
1 onion, chopped	2 cups milk, warmed
1 green bell pepper, chopped	3 cups cooked macaroni noodles
1 mild green chile pepper, chopped	Salt and pepper, as much as you like
1 quart canned tomatoes, chopped	1 cup shredded Cheddar cheese

Turn on your oven to 375 degrees. Lightly grease up a casserole dish.

Brown the sausage in a little hot fat and drain off the grease. Add the onions and peppers and cook for a minute or two on medium-high heat. Turn the heat to medium-low and add the tomatoes, chile powder, and milk and cook for a bit. Add your noodles. Then, salt and pepper it the way you like it.

Pour into the casserole dish and top with the cheese. Cover lightly with foil and bake for about 20 minutes. Remove the foil and bake for another 5 to 10 minutes, or until the cheese is bubbly.

Sprained Ankle Remedy

West Virginians love their sports and they have a special place for the sport of gymnastics. (Our very own Mary Lou Retton is from Fairmont, W.V.) As a young girl, I was very active in gymnastics and infamous for turning up with yet another sprained ankle. Mom would march into the kitchen, get out a paper bag, and tear it into large strips. Then she'd soak the strips in cider vinegar, wrap up my ankle in the wet paper, and then wrap it in a storebought elastic ankle wrap. I'd then have to sit there until it dried or the person sitting next to me passed out from the fumes, whichever came first. Yet, after several hours, the swelling would reduce. Try this little number on your next swollen ankle and you'll see that it really works.

SWEET DADDY'S VEGGIE SOUP

3 large beef ribs

4 bouillon cubes

2 large (28-ounce) cans
   whole tomatoes

1 (8-ounce) can tomato sauce

Pinch of paprika

1 teaspoon Italian seasoning

1 teaspoon crushed red chile peppers

1 teaspoon dried basil

1/2 teaspoon dried oregano

1 clove garlic, minced

2 tablespoons Worcestershire sauce

2 bay leaves

Salt and pepper, as much as you like

5 to 6 large Idaho potatoes,
   peeled and diced

4 to 5 stalks celery, diced

2 large onions, diced

1 package frozen lima beans

1 (15-ounce) can green beans, drained

1 (15-ounce) can corn, drained

1 (15-ounce) can hominy, drained

Get out a deep pot and cook the ribs and bouillon cubes in 5 to 6 cups of water for about 30 minutes. Add your tomatoes, tomato sauce, spices, garlic, Worcestershire sauce, bay leaves, and salt and pepper the way you like it and cook it all for another 30 minutes. Next, toss in your potatoes, celery, and onions and cook another 30 minutes. Last, add your frozen and canned vegetables and simmer until done, about 10 minutes. Take out your bay leaves and toss 'em. Take your ribs out and let 'em cool a bit. Then remove the meat from the bones and put your meat back into the pot. Throw away your bones or save 'em for your hound dog. Serve your soup up hot with some biscuits or a slice of warm, homemade bread.

Poison Ivy Remedy

Simple remedy: If you get poison ivy on you, cover your rash with white shoe polish until all the itchin' goes away.

I tried this one on my husband, Tim, after he had gotten a little too slap-happy cuttin' back the bushes in the backyard. I covered him in shoe polish just like the remedy said. The poison ivy seemed to wane a bit after a day or two, but Tim progressed to smelling like an old leather shoe for a good week.

15 BEANS IN THE POT

Okay, so we Southerners love our beans. They're inexpensive, delicious, and they keep your tummy in good working order. With this recipe, no single bean will do. You need a full fifteen different beans for this soup, which, luckily, come in a premixed bag at most grocery stores. But make sure you throw away the fake ham seasoning packet. You won't need it since you're gonna make up these beans with a slug of real, salted fatback.

1 (20-ounce) package of 15-bean soup
2 quarts water
Small slug of salt fatback, or 1 meaty pork rib
2 (14¹/₂-ounce) cans Southwestern-style or regular diced tomatoes
1 (15-ounce) can tomato sauce

Canned tomato juice, for thinning soup
1 bay leaf
2 tablespoons Worcestershire sauce
Pinch of chile powder
1 teaspoon horseradish
Salt and pepper, as much as you like

Place your beans and water in a big cooking pot and cook at medium-low heat. Put your seasoning meat in a microwavable coffee cup with 4 to 6 ounces of water. Microwave on high for 30 seconds. Turn the meat over and do the same for another 30 seconds. Pour the meat and broth directly into the cooking beans and cook for about 1 hour and 15 minutes, or until the beans are a little over half done.

Next, add the rest of your ingredients to the soup. Simmer on medium-low for another 30 minutes, and then try a spoonful or two to taste for doneness. The beans should be a little firm and crunchy, not mushy. Serve up your beans with a big fat wedge of home-made cornbread and you've got yourself a meal fit for a West Virginia king.

OLD TOM MORRIS'S ROASTED
ROOT VEGETABLE STEW

4 tablespoons olive oil

1 teaspoon ground nutmeg

Salt and pepper, as much as you like

$3/4$ pound rutabagas, peeled and
diced into $3/4$-inch cubes

$3/4$ pound turnips, peeled and
diced into $3/4$-inch cubes

1 fennel bulb, diced into $3/4$-inch cubes

$1/2$ large onion, quartered

1 whole head garlic, top sliced off
(exposing bulbs)

2 portobello mushrooms, cleaned
and cut into $3/4$-inch cubes

5 cups chicken stock

1 (14-ounce) can chopped tomatoes

1 (14-ounce) can white beans,
drained and well rinsed

2 bay leaves

2 fresh sage leaves

1 teaspoon dried savory

Minced fresh parsley, for garnish

Parmesan cheese, for topping

Turn on your oven to 375 degrees. Grease up a casserole dish or baking sheet.

Get yourself out a big bowl and toss in all your vegetables (except the mushrooms) along with 3 tablespoons of the olive oil, the nutmeg, and salt and pepper the way you like it. Spread 'em all out in the pan. Roast in oven for 45 minutes, or until the vegetables start to become tender. Give 'em an extra toss and then add the portobellos. Continue to roast until all your vegetables are tender, about 10 minutes. Set aside.

In a large soup pot, add the rest of the olive oil. Next, add your cooked vegetables (except for the head of garlic) and sauté for about 1 minute. Squeeze out the roasted garlic cloves into your pot. Next, add your stock, tomatoes, beans, bay leaves, sage, and savory. Cook for about 15 minutes, or until the flavors come together the way you like 'em. And don't forget to pick out the bay leaves before serving.

Ladle into soup bowls and garnish with the parsley and Parmesan cheese. If you're feeling a bit Italian, add some cooked pasta at the end.

GIZELLA MAY'S SPOONBREAD

The art of makin' a really great spoonbread lies in the crispy crust that forms from cooking it in a cast iron skillet. If you don't have a cast iron skillet (which you should have), you can always use a glass baking dish, but you just won't get the same special crust. We start by heating up a cast iron skillet until it's nice and hot and then put a tablespoon or two of fat drippings into the pan. While the pan is still warm, pour your spoonbread mixture in. When you hear it sizzle, it's ready for the oven.

1 cup boiling water
1 cup cornmeal
$1/2$ cup milk
$1/2$ teaspoon salt
$1^1/2$ teaspoons baking powder
1 tablespoon butter, softened,
   plus more for serving

2 eggs, beaten
Fat drippings (bacon, sausage, pork,
   or all of them)
Real maple syrup

Turn on your oven to 400 degrees.

Pour boiling water over your cornmeal in a large bowl. Let it cool just a bit. Beat in your milk, salt, baking powder, butter, and eggs.

Heat up your cast iron skillet in the oven until hot. Add a couple of tablespoons of drippings to the skillet and let it fully melt. Pour your spoonbread mixture into the pan and stick it in the oven to bake for 20 to 25 minutes, or until lightly browned on top and slightly puffy. Serve warm with butter and real maple syrup.

Sore Throat "Treatment" #1

Add 1 teaspoon apple cider vinegar to 2 tablespoons water—more vinegar if you can handle it. Gargle it good and for as long as you possibly can. Swallow if you are potassium deficient. You can add honey to this mixture for flavor.

CANNED CINNAMON BUTTER BISCUIT TWISTERS

1 large (10-count) can biscuits (sold in the dairy case, and not the flaky kind)	$^1/_2$ stick butter $^1/_2$ cup sugar 1 to 2 tablespoons ground cinnamon

Separate your biscuits so they can warm up a bit. Melt the butter in a saucepan. In a bowl, combine the cinnamon and sugar. Take 1 biscuit and gently stretch it until it is about $1^1/_2$ inches wide and 6 inches long. Dip in the melted butter and then roll in the cinnamon-sugar mixture. Holding each end of the biscuit, twist the dough about 3 or 4 times and place on a baking sheet. Repeat this process for each of the other biscuits. Bake according to directions on the biscuit can, and serve warm.

MISS EARLIE'S DEE-LIGHTFUL CHICKEN

3 large chicken breasts	$^1/_4$ cup half and half
3 good-sized slices country ham	2 green onions, minced, green
1 (10-ounce) can cream of	parts only
mushroom soup	Pinch of paprika
1 cup sour cream	1 cup shredded Cheddar cheese

Turn on your oven to 350 degrees. Grease up a casserole dish.

Wrap your pieces of chicken with the slices of country ham and place in a casserole dish. Heat your soup, sour cream, and half and half in a saucepan. Bring up to a boil. Pour the soup mixture over chicken. Top with green onions and paprika.

Pop the pan in the oven and bake for 30 minutes. Then take the pan out of the oven and add the cheese. Bake for an additional 15 minutes, or until bubbly.

JEFFRO'S OATMEAL MOLASSES BREAD

1 cup uncooked rolled oats	1/2 cup warm water
1 1/2 cups water	1/4 cup warm molasses
1 teaspoon salt	1/4 cup warm honey
1/3 cup shortening	4 to 5 cups bread flour
1 package active dry yeast	

Microwave your oats and water for about 2 1/2 to 3 minutes on high, or until the mixture bubbles up real good. Add in your salt and shortening, and mix well. Then set aside to cool to about 100 to 110 degrees (just stick in a thermometer to make sure). Get out a large bowl and dissolve your yeast in the warm water. Then pour in your warm molasses and honey. Let the mixture stand for about 15 minutes, or until foamy.

Add the warm oat mixture along with 1 cup of the flour to the yeast mixture and stir it up good. Stir in enough flour to make a medium-stiff dough. Turn your dough out onto a floured surface and knead for about 10 minutes, or until it's fairly smooth. Then stick it in a greased-up bowl. Grease up the top of your dough and cover with a sheet of plastic wrap and a damp kitchen towel. Put in the refrigerator overnight.

Next morning, grease up 2 loaf pans. Push the dough down with the palm of your hand and divide it in half. Put the 2 pieces of dough in the 2 loaf pans, cover with a damp towel, and let them rise in a warm draft-free location until doubled in size (about 1 1/2 to 2 hours).

Turn on your oven to 350 degrees. Bake the loaves for 40 to 45 minutes. You'll know they're done if you tap 'em and they sound hollow.

To make your bread more of a sweet breakfast bread, simply make one of the loaves spicy, nutty, and sweet. When you're rolling out the dough the first time after letting your mixture rise overnight in the fridge, make it about 1/3 inch thick, in the shape of an 8 by 10-inch rectangle. Melt 2 tablespoons butter and spread this over the top of the dough. Mix 1/4 cup each of brown sugar, raisins, and chopped nuts of your choosing with 1/8 teaspoon ground cinnamon. Sprinkle over the buttered dough and roll up jelly roll style. Put this in a greased-up loaf pan, seam side down, and let rise according to directions given for the plain loaves for the second rise. Bake the loaf for 50 to 55 minutes, a little longer than the plain loaf.

Chapter 19

JELL-O SALADS AND OTHER JIGGLY TREATS—ON THE GREATNESS OF SUSPENDED FOOD

In country cookin', gelatin salads (a.k.a. congealed or molded salads) are not considered dessert. They're another side dish to go along with your collard greens, grits, beans, and rolls. Often refrigerated overnight in plastic molds shaped like Christmas trees, flying fish in midswim, or 8-inch-tall rings, gelatin salads have harbored just about everything from 7-Up to sauerkraut. Sometimes they're sweet and sometimes they're savory. Oftentimes they're just plain weird.

I remember having molded salad at just about every major family function. For Christmas, we always had my favorite, Strawberry Banana Congealed Pretzel Salad (facing page), made with cream cheese and fresh strawberry gelatin resting on a crust of crushed pretzels mixed with melted butter. And at church socials, somebody always brought the ubiquitous pale yellow invention made up of gelatin mixed with whipping cream, pineapple, and pimientos. It was often laid out on the table next to the sea foam green gelatin salad and the shiny orange salad filled with an array of mixed fruits forever suspended in a sort of eternal juicy animation.

The great thing about these salads is that they are easy to make and perfect for entertaining since they can be made days in advance. They're jiggly artwork, boasting a creative utilization of color, texture, and flavor. The chef is the artist and the gelatin her medium. So the next time you are looking for a way to wow your family and friends, create a piece of gelatinized art. Inspire those around you with an edible centerpiece. Let your imagination run wild because you're working with two distinct truths when you make these salads: you are the artist, and anything (and I mean anything) can be suspended in gelatin.

STRAWBERRY BANANA CONGEALED PRETZEL SALAD

1 cup crushed pretzels

1 cup crushed graham crackers

1 cup plus 3 tablespoons sugar

3/4 cup butter, melted

1 cup whipping cream

Vanilla extract (optional)

1 (8-ounce) package cream cheese

2 (3-ounce) boxes strawberry gelatin

2 cups boiling water

1 (10-ounce) package frozen
strawberries, thawed

2 bananas, sliced

Fresh strawberries, for garnish

Turn on your oven to 400 degrees.

Your crust comes first. Mix the pretzels, graham crackers, 3 tablespoons of the sugar, and the butter in a bowl. Press your mixture into a glass baking dish and bake for about 8 minutes.

Next, get out your electric mixer and whip up your cream. Add a little sugar and vanilla if you want to get more flavor out of it. Set aside. In your same mixing bowl, beat your cream cheese and the rest of the sugar to combine it. Mix in your whipped cream (remember to save some for the topping) and spread it over your crust. Stick it in the fridge and let it chill until it sets up.

Dissolve your gelatin in the boiling water, and allow to cool just a little. Throw in your strawberries and sliced bananas and then pour the whole shebang over your cream cheese mixture. Refrigerate until it sets up.

Serve your treat with a dollop of whipped cream and some fresh strawberries on the side.

LEMON-LIME SODA–FROSTED GELLY SALAD

For some reason, country folk like to put soda pop in their food. Everything from ice cream, cakes, pies, and gelatin salads often get a sweetened leg-up from a can of cola, ginger ale, or lemon-lime soda. Both the sugar and the effervescence add a weird and wonderful texture that you just can't quite put your finger on.

2 (3-ounce) boxes lemon gelatin
2 cups boiling water
2 cups lemon-lime soda
1 (20-ounce) can crushed pineapple
    (reserve 1 cup of the juice)
2 cups miniature marshmallows
2 large bananas, sliced

2 tablespoons flour
1/2 cup sugar
1 egg, beaten
1 (3-ounce) package cream cheese
1 package Dream Whip
1/2 cup chopped nuts of your choice
Red and green maraschino cherries,
    for decorating

Dissolve your gelatin in the boiling water. Pour in the lemon-lime soda. Then put it all into a glass 9 by 13-inch baking dish or into a fancy gelatin mold and chill until a little syrupy. When it's still a bit mushy, stir in the pineapple, marshmallows, and bananas. Put it back in the fridge and chill until firm.

Combine the flour, sugar, pineapple juice, and beaten egg in a small saucepan. Cook over low heat until thick, stirring constantly. Remove from the heat and stir in your cream cheese. Put it in the fridge again for just a little while.

Prepare the Dream Whip according to package directions. Fold into the cream cheese mixture and spread over the top of the salad. Sprinkle with nuts and chill until ready to serve. Decorate with plenty of maraschino cherries.

BIG WALTER'S RED GELLY SALAD

1 small (8-ounce) can crushed unsweetened pineapple, drained (save the juice)

1 (3-ounce) box strawberry gelatin

$^1/_2$ cup sliced fresh strawberries

2 bananas, sliced

Whipped topping or other favorite toppings on hand

Mix the pineapple juice with enough water to make 1$^1/_2$ cups of liquid. Heat the liquid to boiling and stir in your gelatin. Cool it all in the fridge until the mixture starts to set. Add the pineapple, strawberries, and bananas. Mix it around. Put it back into the fridge until it sets up real firm. Garnish with extra bananas, whipped topping, or any other fruit you can find lying around just before serving.

PINK CHERRY SPONGE SALAD

1 (6-ounce) package cherry gelatin

3 cups boiling water

2 cups cooked rice

Pinch of salt

$^1/_2$ cup sugar

1 teaspoon vanilla extract

1 teaspoon almond extract

$^1/_4$ cup slivered almonds

2 cups heavy whipping cream

Dissolve your gelatin in the boiling water. Stir in the rice, salt, sugar, extracts, and almonds. Chill until just set. Whip up your cream and fold it in, then pour it all into a 2-quart fancy gelatin mold of your choice and chill until set. I like the rooster mold myself.

SHATTERED GLASS CHURCH WINDOW CAKE

Don't let this recipe's name scare you off. This one's a real showstopper, and well worth the two days it takes you to make it since each of your colored gelatins will have to set up in the fridge overnight before they can be incorporated into the actual cake. Imagine the beauty of a stained glass church window meeting up with graham crackers, flavored gelatins, and whipping cream. Take this one to your next potluck and you will blow away the competition.

1 (3-ounce) package orange gelatin
1 (3-ounce) package cherry gelatin
1 (3-ounce) package lime gelatin
3 cups boiling water
1 cup unsweetened pineapple juice
1/4 cup sugar
1 (3-ounce) package lemon gelatin

2 cups cold water
18 crushed graham crackers
3 tablespoons sugar
1/2 teaspoon ground cinnamon
1/2 cup melted butter
2 cups heavy whipping cream

Day one:
Prepare each of your three flavors of gelatin separately using 1 cup of the boiling water for each. Pour each flavor into a separate 8-inch square pan. Chill overnight.

Day two:
Mix the pineapple juice and sugar. Heat until all your sugar is dissolved and remove from the stovetop. Dissolve the lemon gelatin into the hot juice mixture and add 1/2 cup of the cold water. Chill for 30 minutes to 1 hour, until barely thickened.

In another bowl, mix the graham cracker crumbs, sugar, cinnamon, and melted butter. Press the crumbs into the bottom of a 9-inch springform pan. Set aside.

Now, cut your orange, cherry, and lime gelatins into 1/2-inch cubes (you can make them irregular for a real broken glass look).

Next, whip your cream and blend into the lemon gelatin mixture. Gently fold in your cut-up gelatin cubes. Pour the entire mixture into the springform pan. Chill this mixture for at least 5 hours, and preferably overnight.

Remove from the fridge and run a knife or spatula between the sides of the dessert and the springform pan. Carefully unmold your spectacular creation and wow family and friends.

JENKIN JONES'S MOLDED SHRIMP SALAD

1 can tomato soup

2 (8-ounce) packages cream cheese

1^1/$_2$ tablespoons gelatin

1 cup mayonnaise

1 cup chopped celery

^{1}/$_2$ cup minced onion

2 cups mashed-up shrimp

^{1}/$_2$ cup green olives, sliced, for garnish

Mayo, for garnish

Heat up your soup and melt your cream cheese in it. Then add your gelatin. Next, add the rest of your ingredients except your olives. Pour into your Jell-O mold shaped like a flying salmon and chill until set. Unmold your seafood feast on a bed of lettuce leaves and garnish with sliced olives and a big dollop of mayo.

Miss Jane's Illegal Cold Remedy

Mountain people are full of homespun remedies. As a young girl, when I fell ill, I was often "prescribed" some sort of mystery tonic that usually consisted of a select combination of herbs, roots, sweeteners (usually honey), and a few dashes of liquor (often whiskey). I'd pile up on the couch with a mess of vapor rub smeared on my chest, wrapped tightly in a blanket, and drink this piping hot concoction until I "sweat" out the sickness. And you know what? It worked. Every time. Paregoric is available now only by prescription and is an opium derivative. It is considered a narcotic. Use at your own risk!

4 ounces white corn syrup

4 teaspoons whiskey

4 teaspoons paregoric

Take 4 teaspoons every hour.

Chapter 20

LET 'EM EAT CAKE!

FRANCEY'S SMOTHERED-IN-SAUCE APPLE CAKE

1 cup sugar

1 stick butter, softened
  (no substitutes)

1 teaspoon vanilla extract

1 egg

1 cup flour

$^1/_4$ teaspoon salt

1 teaspoon baking soda

1 teaspoon ground cinnamon

1 teaspoon ground nutmeg

4 cooking apples, peeled, cored, and
  finely chopped (about 2 cups)

SAUCE

$^1/_2$ cup sugar

2 tablespoons cornstarch

$^1/_4$ teaspoon salt

2 cups water

$^1/_2$ stick butter (no substitutes)

2 teaspoons vanilla extract

$^1/_3$ cup chopped walnuts

$^1/_3$ cup raisins

Turn on your oven to 350 degrees. Grease up an 8 by 8-inch baking dish.

To make the cake, mix up your sugar and butter and then add the vanilla and egg. Sift your dry ingredients together and add to the creamed mixture. Stir in the chopped apples and pour into the baking dish. Bake for 45 to 50 minutes.

For the sauce, mix the sugar, cornstarch, and salt together, then add the water. Cook until it's thick, stirring often. Remove from the heat and add the butter, vanilla, walnuts, and raisins. Serve the cake warm topped with sauce and enjoy the adulation that will follow.

MISS JESSICA'S LEMON-AID CAKE

1 (3-ounce) package lemon gelatin

$^3/_4$ cup boiling water

1 box yellow cake mix

4 eggs

$^3/_4$ cup vegetable oil

1 small can frozen lemonade, thawed

About $^1/_2$ cup sugar

Turn on your oven to 350 degrees. Grease up a 9-inch tube pan really good.

Dissolve up your gelatin in the hot water and let it cool. Mix up your cake mix, eggs, and oil. Stir in your gelatin. Pour the cake mixture into the tube pan and bake for about 45 minutes.

Mix your lemonade with about $^1/_2$ cup sugar (get it as sweet as you like it). When your cake comes out of the oven, pour on your lemonade mixture and let the cake cool. This cake keeps well in the fridge.

HATTIE'S CHOCOLATE SYRUP CAKE

1 cup flour

1 cup sugar

1 stick butter, melted

4 eggs

15 ounces chocolate syrup

$^1/_4$ teaspoon salt

1 teaspoon baking powder

1 teaspoon vanilla extract

SAUCE

1 cup sugar

$^1/_2$ stick butter

$^1/_3$ cup milk

$^1/_2$ cup chocolate chips

$^1/_2$ cup chopped nuts (your favorites)

Turn on your oven to 325 degrees. Grease up and flour a 9-inch square baking pan.

Mix up all of your cake ingredients and pour into your prepared baking pan. Bake for about 30 to 35 minutes, or until a knife stuck in the center comes out clean.

To make the sauce, put your sugar, butter, and milk in a pan and bring up to a slow boil. Take off the heat and add the chocolate chips and nuts. Pour the mixture over the warm cake.

LUNCH LADY'S OATMEAL CAKE

This cake is one good reason why you should never underestimate the school lunch lady. So what if she spent her working days under one of those half-torn hair nets and the only thing you ever heard her say as you passed the buttered peas was, "You gonna eat that or stare at it all day?" The lunch lady may not have exuded top-shelf social skills, but, man, could she make a mean cake.

1^1/4 cups water

1 cup uncooked oatmeal

^{3}/4 cup white sugar

^{3}/4 cup brown sugar

^{1}/2 cup vegetable oil

2 eggs

1 teaspoon vanilla extract

1^1/3 cups flour

1 teaspoon ground cinnamon

^{1}/4 teaspoon ground cloves

1 teaspoon baking soda

1 teaspoon salt

TOPPING

6 tablespoons butter, melted

^{1}/2 cup brown sugar

^{1}/3 cup canned cream or regular cream

1 teaspoon vanilla extract

1 cup chopped pecans

1 cup shredded sweetened coconut

Turn on your oven to 350 degrees. Grease up a sheet pan.

To make the cake, heat your water to boiling and pour it over the oatmeal. Let it soak for 30 minutes. Add your sugars, oil, eggs, and vanilla to the oatmeal mixture and stir it all real good. Then add the rest of your ingredients and mix everything together. Pour the batter into the sheet pan and bake for 30 minutes.

While the cake is baking, make the topping. Mix together the melted butter, brown sugar, canned cream, vanilla, pecans, and coconut in a medium bowl. Remove the cake from the oven and spread the topping on while it's still hot. Return the cake to the oven for 5 to 10 minutes, or just until the topping starts to bubble all over.

NANNER NUT CAKE WITH CAR MEL FROSTING

This tasty cake gets its special flavor from the addition of "nanners," or as you city folks like to call 'em, bananas. Boasting many typical Southern ingredients, especially buttermilk, this decadent cake is a great way to use up any leftover, overripe "nanners" you might have lying around.

1 cup mashed overripe bananas
1 teaspoon baking soda
1¹/₃ cups sugar
¹/₂ cup butter
2 eggs
2 cups all-purpose flour
1 teaspoon baking powder
¹/₄ teaspoon salt
¹/₂ cup buttermilk
1 teaspoon vanilla extract
¹/₂ cup chopped pecans or walnuts

FROSTING
1 stick butter
1 cup firmly packed brown sugar
¹/₈ teaspoon salt
5 tablespoons milk
2 to 2¹/₂ cups sifted powdered sugar
2 teaspoons vanilla extract

Turn on your oven to 350 degrees. Grease up a sheet pan.

Heat up your mashed bananas and stir in the baking soda. It will be real foamy. Cream your sugar and butter in another bowl and stir in the eggs. Mix together your flour, baking powder, and salt in another bowl and add to the egg mixture, alternating with the buttermilk and the banana mixture. Stir in the vanilla and nuts. Pour into a sheet pan and bake for 25 to 30 minutes. Let cool before frosting.

To make the frosting, heat up your butter in a pan and stir in the brown sugar, salt, and milk. Keep stirring until the mixture comes to a boil. Remove from the heat and gradually add the powdered sugar. Beat until the frosting looks "right" (it should be smooth and creamy). Add more sugar or milk if needed to get a creamy consistency. Add your vanilla and stir well. Now, ice up your cake.

Chapter 21

FRIED PIES, FRUIT PIES, AND CUSTARDS

YOUR BASIC PIE CRUST

Pie crusts tend to be flakier when you don't overwork them and use as little flour as possible. So when you're dusting up your rolling pin and your countertop, always try to go easy on the flour. This recipe makes two 9-inch pie crusts.

2 cups flour, sifted
$^1/_2$ teaspoon salt
1 cup plus 1 tablespoon shortening (use half chicken fat here if you like)
3 to 4 tablespoons ice water, plus more as needed

Mix the flour, salt, and shortening with a fork until it's well blended together. Add the water and mix until a ball forms. To roll out, lightly flour your countertop and rolling pin. Roll out pastry crusts to fit two 9-inch pie plates.

CHICKEN FAT PIE CRUST

Next time you kill and stew a chicken, save the fat drippings by chilling the whole mess. Just spoon off the fat that has congealed on top. Then substitute the fat in your basic pie crust (above). Substitute the chicken fat drippings for half of your shortening. This pie crust is super good when you're baking an apple pie or a mincemeat pie.

WEST VIRGINIA FRIED PIES

One of the best breakfast goodies in the world is a homemade fried pie. Granny used to fry 'em up in a skillet real early in the morning, so we'd awake to the aroma of burnt sugar, cherries, and fried dough. For a little girl like me, there was no sweeter morning treat. We just go ahead and purchase canned pie filling from the grocery store. Cherry works the best and makes your life so much easier.

2 cups flour
4 teaspoons baking powder
1 teaspoon salt
2 tablespoons sugar
$^2/_3$ cup shortening, plus more for cooking
1 large (15-ounce) can evaporated milk (you may not end up using the whole can)
1 (21-ounce) can pie filling (cherry is good, or use your favorite flavor)
Powdered sugar, for dusting

Mix up your dry ingredients. Add in your shortening using a pastry cutter or 2 knives until the mixture forms pea-size nuggets. Using a fork, lightly stir in enough evaporated milk to make a stiff dough ball. Cover the dough and chill for at least 3 hours.

To make the pies, divide the dough into $1^1/_2$-inch balls and roll out into 4- to 5-inch circles. Place a heaping tablespoon of filling on one half of the circle and fold over to look like a half moon. Crimp the edges with a fork. Melt about $^1/_4$ inch shortening in your cast iron skillet and fry your pies until golden brown on each side. Drain on paper towels and sprinkle with powdered sugar.

OVIE CECIL'S CUSTARD GOO

3 eggs
1 cup sugar
$^1/_2$ gallon milk

Pinch of salt
$^1/_2$ teaspoon vanilla extract

Beat up your eggs with the sugar until real creamy. Get out your fancy double boiler and heat it up. Pour in the milk, egg mixture, salt, and vanilla. Cook until you get a custard that coats the back of a spoon. Be sure to stir frequently so your custard doesn't get a yucky "skin" on top. Cool, cover, and put it in the fridge until you finally break down and have to take a bite.

UNCLE JESS'S NUTTY OATS PIE

$^3/_4$ cup corn syrup
$^1/_4$ cup pure maple syrup
3 eggs, lightly beaten
1 cup brown sugar
$^1/_8$ teaspoon salt
1 teaspoon vanilla extract

4 tablespoons butter, melted
$^2/_3$ cup chopped nuts
1 cup uncooked rolled oats
$^1/_2$ cup milk chocolate chips
1 (9-inch) unbaked pie crust (page 154)

Turn on your oven to 425 degrees.

Mix up your syrups, eggs, sugar, salt, vanilla, and butter. Stir in your nuts and oats. Sprinkle chocolate chips over the bottom of your pie crust and pour your filling on top. Bake for about 15 minutes, and then cut your heat down to 350 degrees. Bake your pie for another 30 to 35 minutes, or until it's set up.

MISS MADDY'S JAPANESE FRUIT PIE

Don't let the name of this recipe fool you. There is absolutely nothing Asian in this pie unless you count the coconut, and according to my Aunt Maddy, that's enough to make it Japanese.

1 cup sugar	$^1/_2$ cup chopped dates
2 eggs	$^1/_2$ cup shredded sweetened coconut
1 stick butter, softened	$^1/_2$ cup chopped walnuts
1 tablespoon vanilla extract	1 (9-inch) unbaked pie crust (page 154)
1 tablespoon white vinegar	

Turn on your oven to 350 degrees.

Mix up your sugar, eggs, and butter. Add all the rest of your ingredients and mix well. Pour into an unbaked pie crust and bake for about 45 minutes.

SHOOKS RUN BURNT SUGAR PIE

$1^1/_2$ tablespoons cornstarch	$1^1/_2$ tablespoons melted butter
$1^3/_4$ cups whole milk, cold	1 teaspoon vanilla extract
3 egg yolks	1 (9-inch) pie crust (page 154), baked
1 cup brown sugar, firmly packed	

Make up a smooth paste with the cornstarch and a little of the cold milk. Lightly beat the egg yolks and add to the cornstarch paste. Set aside. Melt up your sugar in a skillet until it is a medium brown color. Scald up the rest of your milk and slowly add to the melted sugar. Cook, stirring constantly to get yourself a smooth, creamy texture. If lumps form, keep stirring until they dissolve. Add the cornstarch paste and egg mixture, the melted butter, and the vanilla. Cook everything together, stirring constantly. Pour into your pie crust and refrigerate. Serve a little cool but not ice cold.

Chapter 22

CANDIES, COOKIES, AND MYSTERY SWEETS

BLACK BOTTOM BANANA BOODLE

This delectable goody is made from a yummy combination of chocolate cookies, banana pudding, and bananas, all layered up in a mushy pile of sweet goodness. Have just one bite and you'll be shakin' your banana boodle in no time! You should be able to find thin chocolate wafers in the ice cream section of your local grocery store.

1 box of thin chocolate wafers (save a few for the crumb topping)	2 cups evaporated milk
	2 cups whole milk
2 boxes of banana pudding mix (not instant)	3 or 4 bananas, sliced
	10 or 12 strawberries, for decoration

Put your chocolate wafers in the bottom of an 8 by 8-inch baking dish, lining the bottom of your dish. Fix up your pudding according to package directions using half evaporated milk and half whole milk. Cool. Stir it now and then so it doesn't get a film on top.

Layer the pudding on top of the cookies, layer on some sliced bananas, more pudding, more chocolate cookies, more pudding, and more bananas until you've used up all you've got. Top with sliced strawberries and cookie crumbs. Cover and chill for at least 4 hours.

PETEY'S ICE CREAM DESSERT

My Aunt Jeanette, who created this recipe, was renowned for her off-color behavior. One of her favorite jaunts was to sneak into the local pool room and drink beer with the guys (an unheard-of behavior in a small, religious town). At the dinner table, her manners weren't a whole lot better. She loved to make this dessert and let her little dog, Petey, lick the ice cream right out of her bowl. When the family chastised her for allowing a dog to eat directly from her dish, Aunt Jeanette would simply exclaim, "Well, why are y'all carrying on? Petey doesn't mind."

70 buttery crackers
3/4 cup chopped nuts of your choice,
   plus more for topping
1 stick butter, melted
2 packages instant vanilla pudding

1 3/4 cups milk
1/2 gallon vanilla ice cream, softened
Sliced bananas
Whipped topping

Mix up your crackers, nuts, and melted butter and press into a good-sized casserole dish to make a crust.

Mix up your pudding and milk and add to the ice cream. Stir it all up together. Pour the mixture into your crust and add a layer of sliced bananas.

Top with whipped topping and sprinkle with chopped nuts. Be sure to let Petey lick your bowl.

WHITE TRASH PEANUT GINGER COOKIES

Dig out a box of your favorite gingersnaps and spread a tablespoon of crunchy peanut butter on each cookie. Press another cookie on top and have yourself a tasty gingersnap cookie sandwich. Great with a glass of cold milk.

APPLE BUTTER HARVEST BARS

Serve up this tasty snack when the leaves start to fall and the apples are hangin' heavy on the trees. This is also a great way to use up some of your homemade apple butter (page 7).

$3/4$ cup butter, softened

$1/2$ cup white sugar

$1/2$ cup packed brown sugar

2 egg yolks

$1^1/4$ cups flour

$1/8$ teaspoon salt

1 cup uncooked rolled oats

1 cup chopped pecans

$2/3$ cup apple butter

Turn on your oven to 350 degrees and grease up a baking dish.

Blend up your butter and sugars. Toss in your egg yolks and beat until fluffy. Mix in your flour and salt and then stir in the oats and nuts. Press half of this mixture into the bottom of the baking dish. Spread the apple butter over the dough to within $1/2$ inch of the edge. Sprinkle with pieces of the extra dough until the surface is evenly coated. Press down carefully but firmly to cover the apple butter. Bake for 20 to 25 minutes, until light brown. Cool and cut into squares.

EDGAR'S HOMEMADE FUDGE

3 cups sugar

$2/3$ cup cocoa

$1/8$ teaspoon salt

$1^1/2$ cans evaporated milk

$1/2$ stick butter, softened

1 teaspoon vanilla extract

Mix up your dry ingredients with the milk and cook over medium heat until it forms a soft ball when you drop a bit into a glass of water. Take it off the heat and add in your butter and vanilla, but don't stir until it cools down to warm. Then, beat it real good until it loses its shine and quickly pour into a buttered dish. Cut into squares and serve.

Chapter 23

BOOZY DRINKS AND
CHURCH-FRIENDLY LIBATIONS

MISS MYRTLE'S HEAVENLY ORANGE DRINK

This recipe is for clean livin', but if you feel like sinnin', you can always add a splash of tangerine- or vanilla-flavored vodka.

6 ounces (³/4 cup) orange juice
  concentrate
1 cup milk
1 cup water

1 teaspoon vanilla extract
¹/2 cup sugar
2 handfuls ice cubes

Blend all your ingredients well in a blender. Serve in fancy glasses at your next church function.

Sore Throat "Treatment" #2

Put a pot of water on the stove. Heat to boiling. Get a teabag of chamomile tea and drop it in a teacup. Pour boiling water over and steep. Add 1 teaspoon apple cider vinegar, 1 teaspoon honey, 1 crushed garlic clove, a pinch of cinnamon, and 1 crushed piece of fresh ginger. Steep some more. Drink hot.

HIGH DOLLAR MOUNTAIN MARGARITA

This is about as fancy as we get when it comes to boozy drinks. It may not be the usual moonshine from a jug, but that still doesn't stop us from bustin' out a little banjo, fiddle, or guitar after downing a couple of these potent treats.

4 ounces Jose Cuervo Especial tequila

2 ounces Grand Marnier

4 ounces frozen limeade
 (^{1}/3 of a 12-ounce can)

4 to 6 ounces water

Juice of ^{1}/2 fresh lime,
 plus lime slices for garnish

Ice cubes

Margarita salt

Get out your fancy tequila, Grand Marnier, limeade, water, and lime juice and mix it all in a wide-mouth quart jar. Add enough ice cubes to almost fill it and stick the jar in the fridge until it's nice and chilled up.

Now, get out 4 margarita glasses and coat the rims in salt. Fill each glass with your chilled margarita mix, adding more ice cubes if you think it needs it. Garnish your glasses with a lime slice.

BLOODSHOTTEN GIN AND GINGER PUNCH

Any real drinking at Granny's house took place in out-of-sight corners of the basement and consisted of a bottle of cheap liquor, a couple of plastic cups, and the company of my Tennessean cousins. This recipe is a good way to dress up a bottle of gin so you don't have to chug it down warm like we did.

1 (16-ounce) package
  frozen strawberries
1 quart ginger ale

1 quart lemon-lime soda
1 large (46-ounce) can pineapple juice
A fifth (750 milliliters) of gin

Toss your frozen strawberries in a large punch bowl. Pour all of your ingredients over the strawberries. Add a little ice if needed. Serve it up nice and cold!

HOT DAMN PUNCH

This is the kind of warm drink that after one good gulp you'll wanna slap your knee and shout, "Hot damn!" Just don't be blasphemin' in front of Granny. Cinnamon liquor (or schnapps) can be found at most liquor stores.

$2^1/4$ cups pineapple juice
2 cups cranberry juice
$1/2$ cup brown sugar
$1^3/4$ cups water
1 teaspoon ground allspice

1 teaspoon whole cloves
3 cinnamon sticks, plus extra for garnish
1 cup (or more) vodka
$1/2$ cup cinnamon liquor (optional)

Percolate all your ingredients together in a crockpot until you can really taste the spices in your cocktail. Serve in mugs with a cinnamon stick for garnish.

GATOR SWEAT

$^1/_2$ pint Southern Comfort (more if you feel like gettin' tanked)
1 large (46-ounce) can pineapple juice
Lemon-lime soda
Lime slices or wedges of fresh pineapple, for garnish

Mix up your SoCo and juice. Pour into glasses filled with ice and top off with lemon-lime soda. Now, stick a big a slice of lime or wedge of fresh pineapple onto the rim of your glass and serve.

WHITE TRASH CHOCOLATE SHAKE

Take yourself a big bowl of vanilla ice cream and squeeze in a bunch of chocolate syrup. Mix it up real well with a spoon. Feel free to lick the spoon at will. Serve up with a side of day-old sweet cornbread.

Sore Throat "Treatment" #3

This sore throat remedy is far less painful to swallow than any using apple cider vinegar. You can crank this one up a notch as my mother often did for me by adding a good-sized tablespoon of Kentucky bourbon. Trust me, it'll put ya right to sleep.

2 aspirins
1 cup hot tea (preferably decaffeinated)
$1^1/_2$ teaspoons honey
Bourbon (optional)

Dissolve the aspirin in the hot tea and add honey. Wrap yourself up in a blanket and drink tea until you start sweating real good.

HEARTBURN LEMONADE

To make a really tasty lemonade, first you gotta make up a sugar syrup. You can use this for all kinds of drink concoctions like limeade or iced tea, and it keeps really well in the fridge. Store your sugar syrup in a jar in the fridge and it'll keep a good while. You can also make this into limeade by using limes in place of the lemons.

4 cups sugar

4 cups water

Juice of 3 to 4 lemons

Strips of rind of 1 lemon or lime

3 to 4 cups cold water, depending on the
size of the lemons/limes

Maraschino cherry, for garnish

Bring your sugar and water to a boil, stirring to dissolve sugar. Cool and store in refrigerator or use immediately.

To make your lemonade, mix up your fruit juice, 1 cup of the sugar syrup (or use more or less, depending on how sweet you like it), and cold water and let it set in the fridge for at least an hour. Then strain it good and pour over ice. Stick a maraschino cherry in each glass to make it fancy.

Tim Morris

ABOUT THE AUTHOR

I was raised on country-fried peasant food. The Golden Delicious apple may be the official state food of West Virginia, but beans, cornbread, stoneground grits, and just about anything cooked up with a big slug of fatback is what makes us who we really are.

My most cherished memories are those precious hours I spent in the kitchen learning West Virginia mountain cooking from my grand-mothers and my mother—rolling out biscuit dough, mixing up a batch of sausage gravy, flipping over fried pies. You could hear the distant sounds of my daddy and uncle pickin' the banjo in the next room, and every now and then, my grandpa would shuffle into the kitchen and dance a little soft shoe while singing "Old Joe's Bar Room" a cappella. We cooked, we gabbed, we ate, and we shared in everything that makes us all want to gather.

It was the original White Trasher, Ernie Mickler, who said it best: "Cooking food, laughing, and storytelling—that's what we're made of and that's what we enjoy the most."